What people are saying about …

Unquestioned Answers

"The whole world is captivated by sound bites and catchphrases. Christians are no exception. With grace and humor, Dr. Jeff Myers peels back the untruth that Christian clichés communicate and helps us marvel at the deep truth of God's Word. *Unquestioned Answers* makes you fall in love with the Bible all over again."

Steve Green, president of Hobby Lobby
and founder of the Museum of the Bible

"There is nothing worse than Christians not thinking Christianly. Believing and repeating sloppy religious clichés hurts the cause of the One who calls us to love him with our whole minds. I thank God for my friend Jeff Myers taking on this vitally important subject. Read it and be blessed and equipped to reach those who are lost and hurting!"

Eric Metaxas, #1 *New York Times*
bestselling author of *Bonhoeffer, If You
Can Keep It,* and *Martin Luther,* and
host of the *Eric Metaxas Show*

"Dr. Jeff Myers has trained tens of thousands of young adults to be leaders. They love and trust him. You'll see why when you read *Unquestioned Answers.* Jeff is a master storyteller who unflinchingly shares his own fears and failures while pointing the reader directly to God. *Unquestioned Answers* is a gold mine of profound truths that go straight to the heart."

Mike Huckabee, former governor of Arkansas, *New York Times* bestselling author, host of *Huckabee* on TBN, and Fox News contributor

"In an age of sound bites, Twitter feeds, and memes, honest-to-goodness conversation and respectful debate are becoming increasingly rare. Critical thinking has become a casualty of these trends—not to mention our understanding of the mystery and depth of the Christian faith. In his compelling new book, Dr. Jeff Myers encourages believers not to answer difficult questions with pat answers and clichés but to rely on Scripture as the ultimate source of truth. This book is sure to change the way many folks view the life-and-death topics we all ponder."

Jim Daly, president of Focus on the Family

"Read this book. Your faith and wisdom will grow, and you'll be brilliantly equipped to help confused and doubting young people. Dr. Jeff Myers will challenge you and make you think. I needed to read this book and you do too."

Kathy Koch, PhD, founder and president of Celebrate Kids Inc. and author of *Screens and Teens*

"Dr. Jeff Myers coined the term *Simplicism* to explain the human tendency to settle for mental shortcuts. *Unquestioned Answers* shows that thinking well is a lot more fun and a lot more life changing. I highly recommend this book."

Del Tackett, host of
The Truth Project

"We *must* teach the next generation of Christians to confidently handle today's culture's challenges, even those that come from inside the church. Jeff Myers, at the helm of Summit Ministries, clears away the confusion surrounding ten trite truisms that are often used as Band-Aids to cover up shallow thinking. *Unquestioned Answers* will help believers of any age become capable agents of change for the kingdom."

Gregory Koukl, president of Stand
to Reason and bestselling author of
Tactics and *The Story of Reality*

"Simplistic Christian platitudes can often do more harm than good—not because they are mistaken but because they are misleading. The tragic result minimizes the mysterious beauty of the gospel and dilutes its life-giving truth. Dr. Jeff Myers is a gifted communicator who challenges the dangerous tendency to offer bargain-basement answers to billion-dollar questions and returns us to the truth of Scripture that is as profound as it is practical."

Matt Heard, lead pastor of Northland
Church, founder of THRIVE, and
author of *Life with a Capital L*

"Every chapter in this book makes me want to shout, 'Yes! Amen!' Dr. Jeff Myers absolutely nails the problem with overly simplistic

Christian mantras that are pervasive today, yet he does so in a beautifully gracious way—no one will walk away from this book feeling guilty for having held these ideas. Instead, you'll walk away inspired to think more deeply about what you believe, why you believe it, and what the Bible *really* says about some of the most important topics today. I can't recommend it enough!"

Natasha Crain, speaker and author of
Keeping Your Kids on God's Side and
Talking with Your Kids about God

"In *Unquestioned Answers*, Dr. Jeff Myers tackles ten popular Christian slogans, turning each one into an opportunity to grow past superficial catchphrases and develop a mature biblical worldview. It's brutally honest yet dripping with grace."

J. Warner Wallace, cold-case detective
featured on *Dateline*; author of *Cold-Case
Christianity, God's Crime Scene,* and *Forensic
Faith*; and creator of the Case Makers Academy

"In *Unquestioned Answers*, Dr. Jeff Myers creatively and thoughtfully shows how common Christian clichés fail to reflect the true biblical picture. But he doesn't leave us there. Weaving together fascinating stories and biblical insights, Myers takes the reader right to the heart of the Bible's wisdom. I highly recommend this book for anyone wanting to live the Christian life with both love and truth."

Sean McDowell, PhD, professor at
Biola University, speaker, and author

"Sometimes clichés catch on because they're true. More often, they catch on because they're easy but poor substitutes for truth. *Unquestioned Answers* is a friendly, thoughtful call to reject faith-deadening clichés and embrace the robust truth of Scripture."

John Stonestreet, president of the
Colson Center for Christian Worldview,
bestselling author of *A Practical Guide
to Culture*, and host of *BreakPoint*

"In *Unquestioned Answers*, Dr. Jeff Myers takes readers below the surface to expose the beauty, goodness, and truth of God's Word. Myers shows us that God does not condemn believers for wrestling with doubts, though we must not forget to doubt our doubts. In addition, the best context to wrestle with our unquestioned answers is in the context of the local church."

Christopher Yuan, speaker and
author of *Out of a Far Country* and
Holy Sexuality and the Gospel

"Reading *Unquestioned Answers* made me crave truth. Jeff Myers vulnerably lets the reader inside his life in a way that made me excited to explore the gospel all over again and share it with others."

Rev. Derek McCoy, media commentator,
pastor, and urban-renewal activist

Unquestioned
Answers

*Rethinking Ten Christian Clichés
to Rediscover Biblical Truths*

Jeff **Myers**

DAVID **C** COOK™

transforming lives together

UNQUESTIONED ANSWERS
Published by David C Cook
4050 Lee Vance Drive
Colorado Springs, CO 80918 U.S.A.

Integrity Music Limited, a Division of David C Cook
Brighton, East Sussex BN1 2RE, England

The graphic circle C logo is a registered trademark of David C Cook.

The website addresses recommended throughout this book are offered as a
resource to you. These websites are not intended in any way to be or imply an
endorsement on the part of David C Cook, nor do we vouch for their content.

Details in some stories have been changed to protect
the identities of the persons involved.

Unless otherwise noted, all Scripture quotations are taken from the ESV® Bible
(The Holy Bible, English Standard Version®), copyright © 2001 by Crossway, a
publishing ministry of Good News Publishers. Used by permission. All rights
reserved. Scripture quotations marked HCSB are taken from the Holman Christian
Standard Bible®, copyright © 1999, 2009 by Holman Bible Publishers. Used by
permission. Holman Christian Standard Bible®, Holman CSB®, and HCSB® are
federally registered trademarks of Holman Bible Publishers; KJV are taken from the
King James Version of the Bible. (Public Domain.); NASB are taken from the New
American Standard Bible®, copyright © 1960, 1995 by The Lockman Foundation.
Used by permission. (www.Lockman.org); NIV are taken from THE HOLY
BIBLE, NEW INTERNATIONAL VERSION®, NIV® Copyright © 1973, 1978,
1984, 2011 by Biblica, Inc.® Used by permission. All rights reserved worldwide.
The author has added italics to Scripture quotations for emphasis.

Library of Congress Control Number 2019948024
ISBN 978-1-4347-1126-7
eISBN 978-0-8307-7204-9

© 2020 Summit Ministries

The Team: Stephanie Bennett, Rachael Stevenson,
Kayla Fenstermaker, Susan Murdock
Cover Design: Nick Lee
Cover Photo: Getty Images

Printed in the United States of America
First Edition 2020

1 2 3 4 5 6 7 8 9 10

010620

*To David Noebel, Paul Stanley, Bernie Kuiper,
Carter Johnson, John Stonestreet, and Matt
Heard, for helping me find robust answers
to perplexing questions and robust questions
worthy of the perplexing answers I found.*

Contents

Acknowledgments

As Summit Ministries' president, I lead a team that prepares young leaders to stand for truth amid gale-force winds of cultural deceit. Everyone in the organization plays a role in a project like this: support services, advancement, programs, and, of course, publishing. Thank you especially to Jason Graham, who refused to let me "phone in" any aspect of this book. Keith Wall banished professor-speak and helped breathe life into each story. Aaron Klemm guided and improved every aspect of this project, from content to marketing. Tosha Payne and Jeff Wood took on an inordinate amount of additional responsibility—I will never know how much, really—to free up my time to write. Julie Ambler guided the Summit Ministries board to make it a priority for me to write books.

Our Summit Ministries faculty includes seventy-five engaging and whip-smart communicators who love Jesus and absolutely will not abide shallow thinking. Their brilliant teaching and dialogue with students inspired this book. From their social media pages, you'd guess that they're a random assortment of professors, entrepreneurs, amateur photographers, talking heads, trail runners, surfers, motocross enthusiasts, and car nuts. Don't let that fool you. They are thought-leaders who are shaping our times.

I think aloud (which is why I should never run for political office), so those who dialogued with me about ideas in this book had a tremendous influence. Thank you especially to Stephanie Myers, Sid Verdoorn, Dan Hodges, John Stonestreet, Verne Kenney, and Graham Myers.

Thanks to Karl Schaller, who helped get the productive relationship between Summit Ministries and David C Cook off the ground. And thanks to Stephanie Bennett, my editor at David C Cook, who has been the calm in the storm throughout many turbulent times.

Introduction

Unanswered Questions, Unquestioned Answers

Every head turned to watch as I made my way down the aisle and dropped into my seat, red faced.

My fourth-grade teacher, Miss Wright, with her bobbed hairdo and perma-tan from years spent as a missionary in Hawaii, fixed her gaze on me, waiting for an explanation.

"Sorry I'm late," I stammered. "Our car wouldn't start."

This was my regular excuse. Our bright orange and pastel white Volkswagen van never started when we needed it to. Like so many other things in those hippie times of the sixties and seventies, the van was cool, charming, and utterly unreliable.

Being late that day reinforced the misery I was already feeling in my first year at a new school. My parents had transferred me to the strict Christian institution when they discovered I wasn't learning anything at my old school in our blue-collar Detroit suburb. I can understand why they moved me. My best friend, Phillip, and I had perfected the art of pilfering our frazzled teacher's answer book as she wandered the room, trying to keep thirty-five rowdy and unmotivated students under control. Getting good grades was easy if you could copy all the answers before getting caught.

But now, in my new Christian school, I was flailing and feeling very out of place.

Glancing around, I noticed a pretty girl, Shelly, mirroring Miss Wright's disapproving glare. My feelings about Shelly were mixed. I couldn't deny she was cute, but I hated when she was chosen to be the classroom monitor—as she always was.

You never caught a break with Shelly. Earlier in the year, I had accidentally tripped her when we left our seats simultaneously to approach the teacher's desk.

"He tripped me!" she fumed. "On *purpose!*"

It wasn't true, but it was hard to stop grinning even as I issued my denials.

Now here I was being scorned again. *Well,* I thought, *there are worse things than being late.* I slipped off my coat and pulled out my math book without looking up at Miss Wright.

Finally, she broke the silence. "Okay, class, get back to your lesson, and I'll come around to collect your homework."

Relieved, I rustled through my briefcase, a little red-and-black plastic satchel my grandfather had given me. I retrieved my homework just as Miss Wright arrived at my desk.

I handed the wrinkled papers to her, knowing exactly what would happen next. Miss Wright would ask the boy next to me, Brian, "Do you have your homework for me?"

Brian would shake his head.

"All right, then. Go to Mrs. Greeley's office," Miss Wright would say.

It happened nearly every day. Brian would push up his glasses on his nose and shuffle toward the door. Some of the girls probably felt sorry for him. The boys were unsettled that he was targeted for daily humiliation. But none of us wanted to be the next Brian. We stared at our books and pretended not to hear the exchange.

Those who had visited the principal's office knew that every problem had the same solution. Proverbs 13:24, King James Version, might have been our school motto: "He that spareth his rod hateth his son: but he that loveth him chasteneth him betimes." Mrs. Greeley interpreted this verse literally. A few swats of a paddle seemed to fix most kids' problems. Just the threat of it kept most of us in line.

After a few minutes the door reopened. Brian shuffled back in and quietly resumed his seat. I glanced over. Tears of resignation rimmed his eyes as he stared blankly ahead. Brian was accustomed to this routine by now, stoically receiving his daily punishment and doing his best to not let anyone see his hurt.

Maybe it was my own frustration at having been late to school for the umpteenth time, but I burned with indignation at Brian's fate. *Has it ever occurred to anyone that a kid who never turns in his homework might have a problem that paddling won't solve?* I wondered.

Suddenly the pattern became clear to my nine-year-old mind. One on one, my teacher and principal were nice. Even Shelly was nice occasionally. Yet the school and its sponsoring church seemed trapped in a rigid system enforced by thunderous pulpit pronouncements: *It's Jesus versus the world. The world wants to drag you into sin. If you doubt, it's because you have a sin problem. If you question what I'm saying, take it up with God* (well-worn Bible held high for emphasis).

Desperate to fit in, I adapted to my situation. I focused more on looking good than doing good. I began to think judgmentally about those who struggled spiritually or academically. I felt pride that I was rarely caught when I did something bad. I usually thought of myself as a basically nice person, but by the end of the school day, I felt mean and sneaky.

No question, my year in Christian school sharpened me intellectually. Our classroom was never out of control and there were no fights in the halls. Nor were there drug dealers lurking on the street corner as they did at my old school. But I was a sensitive kid—the kind who cried when his balloon popped. I dreaded the sternness. I dreaded the backbiting and posturing.

I dreaded the "us versus them" mentality: we are the good guys; everyone else is a fool who will die and go to you-know-where. Chapel messages ended the same way every time: *Are you sure—absolutely sure—that God will find your name in his book when you get to heaven and that you won't be thrown into the lake of fire?*

To be clear, I know there are things we can be certain of. Good and evil exist, and we ought to know the difference and gain the courage to stand for what is true. Yet when everyone you know is an "us" and you don't interact with any "thems," it's natural to wonder whether some among "us" might be "thems" in disguise. Infighting results. As humans, if we don't possess a cause big enough to require unity, we'll tear one another apart. That kind of quarreling over finer points of doctrine and behavior wore me out.

The next year, our family moved out of state. We ended up in the farmlands of Kansas, where my dad joined his family's business. Small-town life was a welcome relief. Friendlier. Safer. We attended a small church where we sang the same songs. That was fine with me because I liked singing. We memorized the same Bible verses. That was fine with me because I loved a challenge. We had youth group. That was fine with me because I liked free food.

But something had changed inside me. I couldn't accept simplistic answers anymore. My doubts about my faith grew, but ironically, so did my judgmental attitude. I judged other believers for thinking they knew the answers. And I judged them for not having answers to my hard questions. Often, I reflected on those people at that small Christian school—Shelly, Brian, Miss Wright, Mrs. Greeley, and all the others. I wondered what they would think about my crisis of faith. Would they admit to having doubts themselves? Finally, I just quit caring. *When I graduate from high school,* I thought to myself, *I'm going to graduate from church at the same time.*

———

My childhood crisis of faith led me to feel that Christianity was a simplistic solution in search of a problem simple enough for it to solve. Christians aren't the only ones who have this issue. Many people today are consumed with a quasi-religious search for simple solutions. They yearn to find easy order in life's complex chaos. And they feel superior when they discover the "obvious" solution others have missed.

We'll call this way of thinking "Simplicism" (SIM-plih-sihz-um). Simplicism is different from simplicity, which is the virtue of living an uncluttered life. Simplicism distorts simplicity into a conviction that something isn't really true unless it is easy to understand and summarize. Bumper stickers are a good example of Simplicism. If there were an award for the town with the greatest bumper-sticker-per-car ratio, my little town in Colorado would surely be a finalist. Everywhere in Manitou Springs, vehicles are plastered with slogans such as "COEXIST" or "#Resist!" or "The left has never been so right" or "Boycott Israel" or "You can't hug a child with nuclear arms."

Bumper stickers—and their counterparts on social media—make Simplicism seem virtuous: "Look at me! I'm a good and brave person for distilling this complex issue down to its essence and righteously taking a public stand."

I make fun, but in truth I'm easy prey for Simplicism's false offer of salvation. I hate clutter. In moments of stress, I obsessively look for things I can throw in the trash. I even discarded my paycheck once and had to retrieve it from the dumpster. When someone promises to reveal a shortcut that gets me to my destination with minimal effort, I'm all in. When someone tells me that all truth can be summarized in 280 characters, I want to believe that person.

Lately, though, I've come to recognize that my attraction to Simplicism is robbing me of the ability to think logically—and speak clearly—about things that matter.

I'm not just concerned for myself. In one of life's ironies, I now head up Summit Ministries, a respected organization that for more than fifty-seven years has inspired rising generations to reawaken their Christian faith and be leaders who stand strong in a culture of great dishonesty. Operating out of a historic hotel nestled at the foot of Pikes Peak, our instructors offer profound insights about the Bible and the big topics everyone is talking about—abortion, socialism, gender identity, pornography, evolution, social justice, and so forth.

We welcome everyone at Summit, but my heart is especially soft toward young adults who have grown up in the church, as I did, but are questioning their faith, just as I did for a season. And that's a large group—two-thirds of young adults who attended church regularly as teens stop attending; less than one-third of those return.[1]

Not only is this a tragedy for the eternal souls of young adults, but it's also a tragedy for our culture. Jesus followers throughout history have transformed the world in science, medicine, human rights, education, the arts, and government. Failing to pass on that heritage puts everything we value as a society at risk.

When I became Summit's president, I carefully studied the characteristics of spiritually at-risk students. My friend David Eaton from Axis helped me find words for the surprising conclusion we reached:

> Some people have *unanswered questions*.
> Far more struggle with *unquestioned answers*.

Unquestioned answers are the way Simplicism banishes doubt. They're the trite slogans and clichés we devise to simultaneously avoid deep thinking and shield our opinions from outside criticism. On the surface, unquestioned answers seem to offer confidence. But in the end, they confuse and isolate us. In this book we'll examine some clichés that Christians believe without really thinking about them. This includes slogans such as "Love the sinner; hate the sin" and "Just have faith" and "It's not my place to judge."

I needed to write this book because I needed to *read* this book. As I wrote, I found myself convicted by the weakness of beliefs I had never taken time to wrestle with. I am full of unanswered questions. But I am also, embarrassingly, full of unquestioned answers. I know I'm not alone. I can't tell you how many people I've journeyed with— especially twentysomethings and thirtysomethings—who lost their footing when a single professor or trusted person called into question a closely held but unexamined belief. Many have yet to recover.

To be fair, we need simple answers for some things. Mental shortcuts help us navigate all the commercial messages, news items, and social media posts bombarding us every day.[2] Simple sayings can help us remember some valuable life rules. The spelling rule "*i* before *e* except after *c*, unless it sounds like *a*" helps me correctly spell words. It has some exceptions, but only a true grammar geek craves something more thorough.

Yet simplifying things so we can think more clearly is different from developing unquestioned answers that stop us from thinking altogether. The first leads to wisdom. The second leads to, well, Simplicism.

Unquestioned answers are on the rise, unfortunately. They're like addictive drugs. It's hard to stop with one hit. And it's a far more dangerous habit than we realize.

The Dark Side of Unquestioned Answers

When I reflect on the unquestioned answers I have believed, I realize that I often hide behind simplistic slogans because they reinforce my beliefs while making me feel more righteous than those with whom I disagree.

But I've come to realize that unquestioned answers can cause at least three serious problems.

Unquestioned answers make us vulnerable. Reality has a way of challenging our simplistic notions. If we don't have the ability to go deeper, we can quickly spiral into discouragement and despair. If you've experienced a tremendous loss, such as divorce or the death of a child, hearing someone say "Just have faith" doesn't help. And if a friend is struggling with addiction, sitting by and telling yourself "It's not my place to judge" will not give her the help she needs.

Unquestioned answers disillusion us. When our unquestioned answers fail to stand up under scrutiny, we become distrustful of those who gave them to us. This often happens in church. The new generation of adults has the lowest level of church attendance of any generation in American history.[3] When churchgoers' surface-level answers fail them, are they prepared to dig deep into the gospel's power? Or has clamoring for easy answers replaced the pursuit of hard truths?

Unquestioned answers produce shame, not change. Unquestioned answers motivate us by making us feel ashamed if we disagree. But this kind of motivation is counterproductive. People who are shamed into agreement usually switch back to their previous opinions once the pressure is off. As the old saying goes, "A man convinced against his will is of the same opinion still."

At their extreme, unquestioned answers shut down vital discussions and turn others away from the truth. One of my friends developed a PowerPoint presentation with a set of "dueling fish" images to illustrate this point. In the first image, a believer puts a Jesus fish on his car. Then his atheist neighbor responds with a Darwin fish. Then the Christian takes off his Jesus fish and replaces it with a Jesus-fish-eats-Darwin-fish. On and on the slides go, until the audience is laughing at the absurdity of it all.

Here's my question: What are the odds that the Christian and atheist dueling with their car decals will ever sit down to discuss their perspectives? Not very good. It's much more likely they'll become cynical and angry and communicate even less.

Unless we learn to think more clearly and dialogue more openly, our society is in for a rough time. Thoughtfulness is vital for everyone. But as a Christian I feel the need to start in house. Jesus followers ought to lead the way.

In a way, this book is about my own journey of faith. I've struggled through many of the clichés we will explore in its pages. When I started writing, I envisioned a quick and easy work that would make me feel clever about what I've learned through the years. I wanted to speak as someone capable of responding to every untruth with a clever retort. Instead, I've been convicted: I have settled for less than the truth nearly every day of my life. In the following pages, I'll reveal how. Some of it is embarrassing, but I just don't know another way to open a thoughtful conversation about misplaced beliefs that keep faith at a shallow level. I'm looking for robust answers to my questions, and questions that are robust enough to deserve the answers I find.

In that hope, here are ten unquestioned answers I'm concerned are keeping us from hearing God's call to go deep.

Christianity's Top Ten Unquestioned Answers

It's easy to slip into accepting unquestioned answers. As my team and I considered a lengthy list of possibilities, we settled on ten that we've heard repeatedly:

1. "God said it; I believe it; that settles it for me."
2. "Just have faith."
3. "God will heal our land if we humble ourselves and pray."
4. "It's just me and Jesus."
5. "Love the sinner; hate the sin."
6. "Christianity is a relationship, not a religion."
7. "Jesus was a social justice warrior."
8. "It's not my place to judge."
9. "This world has nothing for me."
10. "God is good all the time—all the time God is good."

By wrestling with these clichés, I've sensed a change in my own life. My relationship with God is closer. I'm more inclined to ask questions and listen thoughtfully to others. I have a better understanding of the Bible, faith, prayer, Christian community, sin, forgiveness, worldview, justice, judgment, the world, and God's goodness. I hope you'll feel the same way as you journey through the pages of this book.

These changes will help us realize that God expects us to think and reflect well. Jesus told his followers to love God with all their hearts, souls, and *minds* (Matt. 22:37). Paul told his readers that "we have the *mind* of Christ" (1 Cor. 2:16). Peter encouraged Christians to give a reasoned case for what they believe (1 Pet. 3:15). Believers are to study hard (2 Tim. 2:15) and seek wisdom and understanding (Prov. 4:5).

Of course, this doesn't mean that only people with high IQs can grasp Jesus's good news. Jesus said that unless we change and become like little children, we cannot enter the kingdom of heaven (Matt. 18:2–3). Still, Jesus's words don't justify childishness. We are to be mature in our faith (1 Cor. 14:20) and growing more mature all the time (Heb. 5:14).

God even designed our bodies to think hard and enjoy the pursuit of truth. Brain research shows that thinking intensely and reflecting deeply stimulate the pleasure center of our brains, causing a kind of joy so compelling that it's as if we're touching eternity.[4]

I don't touch eternity often, I'm ashamed to admit. I'm easily distracted. I find thinking painful at times. What I need is to blow the dust off my treasure chest of unquestioned answers, open the creaky lid, and bravely face what's inside. It's the only way I'll ever grow in maturity and speak truth in love to an aimless, angry world.

Recovering Belief from Unquestioned Answers

When as a child I began questioning my faith, I felt a sense of annoyance that others hadn't "seen the light." That feeling didn't last. Gradually—very gradually—I realized that my chosen worldview of unbelief was very narrow. It assumed a lot of things about the world that I knew couldn't be proved. It reduced the world to its parts, but it couldn't make me whole.

Finally, I gained the courage to doubt my doubts. That's when I came back to Jesus and realized he wasn't the one keeping me in bondage. Rather, he was the one who could set me free. Once my heart and mind opened to the fullness of Christ, I craved reality, with its clarity and its mysteries, its beauty and its ugliness, its hopes and its fears, its dreams and its disappointments.

If you're skeptical of this, I understand. Believe me. If we were sitting across from each other over cups of coffee, I would want you to feel safe to express how you see things. I'd want to ask you questions about your journey. If I sensed you were open, I'd want to express how hard it has been for me—even as a convinced believer—to engage the ideas that rule the world rather than try to escape them.

When I find myself discouraged by the challenges of faith, I gather hope from watching some of Summit's students living out their beliefs today. I recall Noah—a past Summit student— who was elected student body president at Dartmouth College. In his speech to the incoming freshmen, Noah pointed out that, statistically, the incoming class was "the smartest and most diverse group of freshmen" in Dartmouth's history. But then he went on to tell stories of a Dartmouth graduate who became a murderer, one who became a Soviet spy, and one who sexually assaulted a young girl. Intelligence is not enough, he told his young audience. They needed to be people of character.

To illustrate his point, Noah pointed to Jesus in the garden of Gethsemane and said that Jesus "knew the right thing to do. He knew the cost would be agonizing torture and death. But he did it anyway. That's character."

Noah's point landed like a spark on the dry tinder of today's politically charged culture. The resulting firestorm was predictable. Noah's words were called "disrespectful," "appalling," and "reprehensible." He was accused of abusing his position of power and embarrassing the student government by mentioning Jesus Christ at an institution of higher learning.

What Noah did next is something no one expected. He reached out to his critics one by one and listened to their concerns.[5] Developing an impulse to engage rather than escape difficult situations has served Noah well. Now in his thirties, Noah is a successful corporate executive and venture capitalist who invests his free time mentoring young adults at his church.

I also recall Haley—another Summit student—who is now an executive with the National Center on Sexual Exploitation. This group stands against sexually explicit and sexually objectifying content in the media. In the past, people like Haley would have been considered scolds who wanted to impose their morality on everyone else. But in testifying before the United Nations, the Department of Justice, the Department of Health and Human Services, and the FBI and in speaking with media outlets such as the *New York Times* and Fox News, Haley has taken an unexpected approach. She shows that sexually oriented advertising and programming are part of a complicated web of harmful practices that result in the exploitation of women and children.

As a result of the work Haley and her team have done, Google has stopped offering sexually explicit ads and removed pornographic apps from Google Play. Steam—one of the largest distributors of video games—now rejects games that include sexually graphic content. *Cosmopolitan* magazine has been removed from checkout lines at Walmart. Revcontent, one of the world's largest internet advertising networks, has removed sexually explicit and sexually objectifying content. Congress has passed historic legislation to fight sex trafficking. And Hilton, Crowne Plaza, Westin, and many other top hotel chains have stopped distributing on-demand hardcore pornography in their guest rooms.

Haley's work is strongly rooted in her Christian faith. Yet even people whose political and social views are at odds with her own seek her advice. Though just twenty-six at the time of this writing, Haley has been asked by the mayor of Washington, DC, to offer recommendations for improving child welfare and stopping child abuse.

Haley says her training at Summit Ministries helped her connect the dots between ideas and actions. She learned to think critically about the worldviews behind people's actions and the policies governing our nation. It's about people, not just ideas. It's about relationships, not just truth.

The more divisive and angry that society becomes, the more refreshing the approaches taken by Noah and Haley seem. They've tapped into something deep about how to think and communicate the truth. They're making a difference because of—not in spite of—the compelling answers their faith provides to the most pressing issues of our time.

And yet there's a good reason I don't have thousands of stories like Noah's and Haley's to share. What they're doing is *grueling*. It involves hard thinking about reality, God, the Bible, faith, and church. It requires abandoning our unquestioned answers and navigating the tension between longing to be with Jesus and living in a way that makes a difference.

What You'll Learn along the Unquestioned Answers Journey

Like the students I work with at Summit, I'm on a journey. Yes, I head up a ministry. Yes, I have been to graduate school and have written other books. But what qualifies me to write *Unquestioned Answers* is that I'm walking alongside those I lead. I know what it feels like to be given overprocessed and prepackaged answers. I know how tempted I am to settle for the easy solution, and I don't like it.

What I want is to forsake my unquestioned answers and awaken again to the wonder of God, the Bible, and the world he made.

This book can help us

- know that the Bible is true and what it means when we say that;
- stop being at a loss for words in conversations about our faith;
- experience a fresh vision for church;
- act wisely in a culture that encourages foolishness;
- speak the truth without being judgmental;
- apply the wisdom of the Bible to everything everywhere all the time.

Along the way we'll encounter a lot of quirky people whose journeys have shed light on our own paths, from a Christian businessman who decided to confront liberal theology and sparked a global movement ... to Irish monks who inadvertently transformed education by setting out on pilgrimages ... to an Oxford professor named "Fat Head" who triggered the development of modern science ... to a writer who changed a nation by penning an encyclopedia ... to an American poet who, overcome by despair, wrote a famous hymn that brought hope to a nation bent on self-destruction.

When I look back on that hurt, resentful nine-year-old boy moving from Michigan to Kansas, I reflect on where my faith journey has taken me. My first step took place shortly after that childhood move to Kansas, when my brother and I built a bomb in the church parking lot. It's an odd place to begin, I know, but it started a series of events that introduced me to the amazing truth of God's Word.

Discussion Questions

1. How does Simplicism differ from simplicity?

2. How would you describe the effects of Simplicism on our culture? On your life?

3. What are some clichés that you have found yourself reciting without having reflected on them?

4. What clichés are you looking forward to reading about? Why?

For videos, additional related Scripture passages, further reading, and more content specific to each unquestioned answer, visit www.unquestionedanswers.com/resources.

1

"God Said It; I Believe It; That Settles It for Me"

Rediscovering Truth about the Bible

When I was nine, our family packed our belongings into a sixteen-foot U-Haul truck, Volkswagen van in tow, and set out across the country. After three days of hundred-degree weather, creeping along at the federally mandated fifty-five miles per hour that drove everyone crazy in the 1970s, we arrived at our new home, a mercifully air-conditioned little saltbox house in a well-kept Kansas neighborhood.

Our new small town, Great Bend, had experienced an oil boom, resulting in well-funded schools, broad streets, parks, and a well-equipped hospital. Unlike in Detroit, my parents didn't mind letting their kids roam. So my brother, Scott, and I explored every inch of our neighborhood by bicycle.

It was culture shock to move from a city of 1.5 million people to a town of sixteen thousand. Even more startling was the transition from a church of two thousand, with thriving ministries for every age-group, to a country church so small that our family of five increased attendance by 20 percent.

Our tiny new congregation offered no youth program, so during the Wednesday evening prayer meeting, Scott and I just played outside. One evening, as we explored the property, we tried the door of a shed and found it unlocked. We peered inside. And what did we find? A lawn mower.

"Are you thinking what I'm thinking?" I asked Scott.

"If there's a lawn mower, there must be gasoline?" he replied.

"Exactly."

Excited, we tiptoed into the church basement to find supplies: paper cups, masking tape, and matches. Carefully we stitched together a "bomb" and lit it in the half-empty parking lot. It's a wonder we didn't burn our hair off. As it blazed, our cup-and-tape contraption tipped over and spilled. We quickly cleaned up the mess and threw the evidence in a trash can.

We didn't think anyone had noticed, but to our surprise, the next week there was a youth group! It consisted of three boys: Scott and me, along with Burton, the son of the town's police chief. Our leader, Don, got down on his knees to pray and encouraged us to do the same. We knelt there in awe, eyes mostly screwed shut, as Don spoke to God with reverent confidence. What started out as a means of keeping us out of trouble blossomed into a mentoring relationship that affected our lives for decades to come.

A few years ago Don and I visited shortly before his death from cancer. We sat together at the dining room table to chat, cry, and pray, knowing it would be our last meeting this side of eternity. At the end of our visit, I grabbed my jacket, and Don's wife, Angel, took my arm.

"I want to show you something," she said.

We walked over to the fireplace, where she pointed out a grease stain on the brick hearth.

"Do you know how that got there?" she asked.

"I have no idea," I replied.

"When this fireplace was brand new," Angel informed me, "you and Scottie decided to cook hot dogs on it. They burst and dripped this grease, and it never came out."

"I'm so sorry," I blurted.

"I'm not trying to make you feel bad," she quickly replied. "I just want you to know that every time we see that stain, we pray for you boys."

Imagine that. For thirty-five years this couple had prayed for my brother and me every time they came near their fireplace. Both Scott and I are in full-time ministry today. Only in heaven will we know how many pitfalls we avoided and how many spiritual battles were won as Don and Angel stood in prayer in their tiny living room.

I'm sure it wasn't easy for them. Every week, I pestered Don with questions. "That church across town—what do *they* teach?" I would ask. "And how do we know we're right and they're wrong?" Some of my questions were more pointed: "How do we really know God exists?" "Do we need to obey *everything* in the Bible—even the Old Testament commands?" "How should Christians respond to philosophers who doubt God exists?"

Don admitted that his journey with Jesus had bypassed street-level debates about theology and philosophy. Plus, he had a hard job and a wife and four daughters to care for, so there wasn't much time to look for answers.

Something our pastor said one Sunday, though, stuck in my mind as an example of how Christians typically grapple with hard questions. After making what he seemed to think was a rather strong sermon point, he held up his Bible and said, "If you don't like it, don't take it up with me. Take it up with God. God said it, I believe it, and that settles it!"

Even as a kid, I suspected something was amiss with that kind of logic. There was no room for discussion, and asking questions seemed akin to disrespecting God himself. But I had a hard time believing that it was actually sinful for women to wear jeans and for men to have long hair, that alcohol in moderation was actually bad, or that the King James Version of the Bible was the only authorized translation.

For many years I marveled at how people like my pastor could arrive at such strong convictions through Bible passages that seemed unclear to me. I thought, *Why do I have such a hard time seeing what seems obvious to people I trust?*

The answer came to me years later when I was writing *Understanding the Faith*, a textbook about theology and apologetics used in Christian schools. Acknowledging my lack of theological training, I asked several trusted theologians to write research papers to help me sort through tough questions about God, the Bible, sin, creation, morality, hell, and other faith topics.

Reading those papers, I felt like a hillbilly on his first visit to the big city. For most of my life, I had studied the Bible one passage at a time to answer the question "How does this apply to my life today?" I had been peering through a keyhole when God wanted to swing the door wide open and reveal all of reality. The Bible is a book about everything, and it applies to everyone everywhere. As such, it is transformational, psychologically insightful, historically accurate, literarily brilliant, and inspired.

Understanding the Bible's bigness reinvigorated my faith. The broad scope of God's plan for the world took shape in my mind, dimming my obsession with what *I* believe and what "settles it for *me*." I decided to embrace the challenge of viewing the Bible as special revelation from God and seeing the world through its telescoping lens.

Where Does This Unquestioned Answer Come From?

Remember when Thomas refused to believe that Jesus had risen from the dead until he had touched Jesus's crucifixion wounds? Jesus invited Thomas's touch but chided him, saying, "Blessed are those who have not seen and yet have believed" (John 20:29).

No one wants to be a doubting Thomas. The message I absorbed growing up was that questioning is doubting, and doubting is sinning. As a prominent Christian leader asserted, "Of all the sins we can commit, doubt is the one most hated by God."[1] If that's true, I committed the greatest sin even at a young age. It was only after high school when I arrived at Summit Ministries that I turned a corner, but that's a story for later in this chapter.

Those who believe we should unquestioningly accept the Bible as God's Word often enlist the famed nineteenth-century preacher Charles Spurgeon, who proclaimed, "The Word of God can take care of itself, and will do so if we preach it, and cease defending it.... Let the pure gospel go forth in all its lion-like majesty, and it will soon clear its own way and ease itself of its adversaries."[2] Defending the Bible strips it of its true power. Don't try to logically understand it; just unleash it.

This way of thinking inspired a Christian song popular when I was a kid: "God Said It; I Believe It; That Settles It." I recently found an early music video of it that featured women in pale-pink dresses and men in powder-blue suits and white patent-leather shoes. They lyrics state, "Though some may doubt that His Word is true, / I've chosen to believe it; now how about you?"[3]

Freeing, right? We don't need to know why the Bible is true—we just need to believe it.

Interestingly, the Bible itself doesn't take this perspective. The Bible claims to be inspired by God and true in its claims about God and his creation, but it also calls for examination of its claims. Can the Bible stand up to our questions, or should we just believe it and stop asking them?

Why We Say the Bible Is God's Word— and How We Can Know It Is True

The Bible contains rules, but it's not helpful to think of it as a rule book. As important as rule books are, they don't inspire devotion. Imagine curling up with a cup of coffee and your company's employment manual. Good times, right?

Instead of a rule book, think of the Bible as a compass. When my children and I tested for our advanced open-water diving certification, we descended to forty feet below the surface and took turns swimming in a square, a hundred feet in each direction. At the farthest point, we were about 140 feet from the rest of our group in an environment where visibility was fifty feet at best. Believe me, at that moment I didn't want a compass that pointed at *me*; I wanted one that offered a reliable reference point outside me. Only then could I find my way back.

Just as a compass points us north, the Bible points us to God. It reveals God, making the unknown known. Through revelation, God's truth rises like the dawn, making clearer who God is, who we are, and what kind of world we live in. The Bible is God's Word.

Saying this doesn't mean the Bible magically fell from heaven leather bound, as my friend Jonathan Morrow whimsically phrased it.[4] Rather, the Bible was assembled through a human and divine process. When we say the Bible is God's Word, we're saying it is inspired by God and that what it claims as true is indeed true.

Second Timothy 3:16 says, "All Scripture is *breathed out by God* and profitable for teaching, for reproof, for correction, and for training in righteousness." The Greek word for "breathed out by God" is *theopneustos*. It means "inspired by God." To say Scripture is inspired is to say that what its authors wrote was precisely what God himself wanted to be communicated.

About three thousand times in the Bible, the various writers claim to have been guided by the Holy Spirit.[5] The stunning result is a completely coherent book made up of sixty-six separate books written over the course of 1,500 years by forty writers, from kings and philosophers to fishermen and tentmakers … yet all the pieces fit together.

Many theologians go beyond *inspiration* to also say that the Bible is without error, or *inerrant*. This doesn't mean no errors were made in transmitting the text through time. It means that when Scripture is carefully interpreted in light of the culture in which it was written and the means of communication common to that time, it is completely true in what it says about God and his creation.[6] There is a great deal of evidence for both claims—that the Bible is inspired by God and that it is without error. This evidence comes internally from the Bible itself and externally from scholarly investigation.

Internal Evidence for the Bible's Claims

Internally the Bible claims authority for itself. Since Jesus is at its center, most evangelical theologians start with Jesus and work their way backward and forward. Looking backward, we see that Jesus treated the Old Testament as authoritative. In his earthly ministry, Jesus claimed authority (John 5:22). Looking forward, we see that Jesus granted his own authority to the apostles whose ministry carried on after his resurrection (Matt. 28:18–20).

Jesus didn't treat the Old Testament as past. He referred to it as the eternal truth of God. The Gospels contain many examples of Jesus quoting from the Old Testament. When Jesus quoted Scripture, he used the perfect tense ("it is written" or "it stands written"). These teachings are not simply in the *past*, Jesus was saying; they are for *now*.[7]

Further, Jesus claimed not only to be God's spokesman but also to be God in the flesh. In contrast to the Old Testament prophets who said, "Thus says the LORD," Jesus said, "Truly, truly, *I* say to you." He manifested divine authority to reveal what God wants us to understand.[8] Jesus claimed to be the I AM of the Old Testament (John 8:58). He said that he and God are one essence (10:30) and that those who had seen him had seen God (14:9). Jesus claimed authority over heaven and earth, including the power to judge (5:22).

Jesus's claims astonished his audience, his enemies, and his disciples.[9] They astonish us today too and leave us with a choice. Many people appreciate Jesus's *decency* but not his *divinity*. They approve of his teachings but not of his claim to be God. As we have seen, though, Jesus did not claim to be only a good moral teacher. He claimed that his words were God's words.

As far as the rest of the New Testament is concerned, Jesus conferred authority on those he had personally encountered before the completion of his earthly ministry. John 14:25–26 says, "These things I have spoken to you while I am still with you. But the Helper, the Holy Spirit, whom the Father will send in my name, he will teach you all things and bring to your remembrance all that I have said to you."

The disciples did just what Jesus said. They proclaimed the good news in Jesus's name (see Acts 3:6, 16; 4:7, 10, 12, 17–18, 30). Even

Jesus's enemies acknowledged the authority with which Jesus's disciples spoke, recognizing that "they had been with Jesus" (Acts 4:13).

External Evidence for the Bible's Claims

Lots of evidence outside the Bible also shows that it didn't proceed from the fanciful imaginations of spiritual people but is based on actual events in history. Because of this, we can use historical evidence to verify that the Bible is true.

Those copying the Scriptures from one generation to the next proceeded with great care, leading us to believe that the Hebrew and Greek manuscripts we have today vary little from the original versions. Beginning in 1947, the Dead Sea Scrolls were discovered in a series of caves in the Judean Desert of Israel. One of those scrolls was the nearly complete text of the book of Isaiah. Scholars dated this scroll as about one thousand years older than the next-oldest copy, yet between the old and the newer versions, there was a variation of less than 5 percent. Most of the differences were just spelling variations and obvious scribal errors.[10]

In the early 1990s the late biblical scholar Philip R. Davies claimed there was no way to know whether King David from the Bible actually existed.[11] But just a year after his book was published, an inscription referring to the "house of David" was found at the Tel Dan archaeological site. Israel Finkelstein, professor of archaeology at Tel Aviv University, remarked, "Biblical nihilism collapsed overnight with the discovery of the David inscription."[12] More recently archaeologists have discovered what they believe to be a palace of David, providing additional evidence for his existence.[13]

So much evidence for the historical accuracy of the Bible now exists that journalist Jeffery Sheler remarked, "We have found the Bible consistently and substantially affirmed as a credible and reliable source of history."[14]

That's not all. Sources outside the Bible—such as Josephus, the Talmud, Tacitus, and Pliny the Younger—demonstrate that Jesus really existed, he was thought to have performed miracles, he was crucified under the authority of a governor named Pontius Pilate, and a community of worshippers grew significantly based on the belief that he was still alive.[15]

Shouldn't this kind of evidence at least cause us to give the Bible the benefit of the doubt?[16]

What Should We Do Now?

Our family station wagon chugged up the narrow streets of Manitou Springs, Colorado.

"This must be the place," my father said, looking up at a quaint antique hotel.

I stared out the window at the sight. At age seventeen and freshly graduated from high school, I felt ready to spread my wings. From the two-week program I was attending, I would go straight to debate camp and then off to college.

We strolled into the dimly lit lobby and came face to face with a tanned, athletic-looking man sporting huge glasses. He introduced himself as Dave Noebel, but everyone called him Doc. I had no idea at the time how knowledgeable he was—I knew only my own desperate search for truth.

"Doc," I said, "I hope you have a lot of answers, because I have a lot of questions."

"Tiger," Noebel replied, using his favorite term of affection, "at Summit we're not afraid of questions."

I couldn't believe it. Asking questions—hard questions—was okay? Seriously? It was nearly the opposite of what I had come to think Christians believed. That was the moment my turnaround began. Like a satellite ever so slightly altering trajectory with the burst of a thruster, I began moving into a new orbit.

Looking back, I can see that those who proclaim "God said it; I believe it; that settles it for me" are casting about for a way to show that their beliefs are based on solid rock, not shifting sand. But the truth is so much more profound than this saying indicates. God's Word doesn't stop our inquiries; it invites them.

Now when people tell me they have questions, I respond, "Good for you. Wrestle with them. Explore them. And don't forget to doubt your doubts as much as you doubt what God says." I say this because the Bible itself calls for believers to be deeply familiar with it (Ps. 119), interpret it accurately (2 Tim. 2:15), defend it (1 Pet. 3:15), and answer arguments against it (2 Cor. 10:5). No other holy book issues an explicit call for careful study the way the Bible does.

The Bible promises several benefits to believers who engage in such study:

1. *Blessing:* delight, freedom from shame, wisdom, hope, and protection against doing evil (Ps. 119:6, 11, 47, 49, 98).

2. *Spiritual fruit:* "love, joy, peace, patience, kindness, goodness, faithfulness, gentleness, self-control" (Gal. 5:22–23).

3. *Freedom from spiritual bondage:* The apostle Paul wrote, "Where the Spirit of the Lord is, there is freedom" (2 Cor. 3:17).

4. *Direction in life:* The book of Proverbs tells us, "In all your ways acknowledge him, and he will make straight your paths" (3:6).

5. *The ability to grasp truth and defeat error:* In 2 Corinthians we read, "The weapons of our warfare are not of the flesh but have divine power to destroy strongholds" (10:4).

From its beginning the Bible has been under attack. It has been picked apart, banned, or mocked by critics. It has been confiscated and destroyed, and its translators have been burned at the stake. God's Word cannot be stopped, but its opponents never seem to learn that.

Often in history, trust in the Bible seemed to revive even amid harsh criticism. One such instance occurred in the early 1900s, a time period that many today think of as Victorian and somehow purer. The truth is, as the nineteenth century turned into the twentieth, truth began falling out of fashion. Theologians climbed all over one another in their haste to explain away the Bible's claims. Evolution disproved the Bible's creation account, they said. Only the naive believed in miracles. The Bible was full of contradictions. Church fathers had omitted gospels that didn't fit their narrative.

Key biblical figures such as King David never existed. And on and on. Firm believers felt under siege. The media portrayed them as ignorant hicks.

A businessman named Lyman Stewart decided to act. He recruited a pastor and a professor to compile essays defending the truth of the Bible and refuting its critics. With Stewart's financial backing, three million volumes of this twelve-volume series, The Fundamentals, made their way to pastors, missionaries, and other leaders around the world.[17]

The response was overwhelming. Hundreds of thousands of people wrote, most expressing gratitude for how The Fundamentals had helped them stand strong. Attendance at biblically faithful churches exploded. This fundamentalist movement transformed into a larger movement—evangelicalism—that included young and old, Democrat and Republican, urban and rural. In the end, it became one of the most successful religious movements in history.[18]

Today evangelicalism has spread to 129 nations and six hundred million people.[19] Evangelicalism is growing twice as fast as Islam.[20] What has taken place is really an extended revival, though it was easy to miss because it was based on convictions rather than emotional ecstasy.

Careful study—or questioning—of the Bible has inspired believers through the centuries to seek a deeper faith. A world-changing faith. The Bible's moral guidance led them to abolish slavery, ban child molestation, seek dignity for women, form hospitals and schools, secure liberty and justice for all, advance science, develop great art and architecture, and protect human life.[21]

The Bible begs to be understood, defended, and applied. And for the record, the famed preacher Charles Spurgeon, the theologian often quoted as denying the need for apologetics, would have agreed with the "defend" part. In an 1888 sermon titled "Holding Fast the Faith," Spurgeon said explicitly, "We must defend the faith; for what would have become of us if our fathers had not maintained it?"[22]

Spurgeon's question left me thinking, *What is faith, really? Is all faith really just blind faith?* As I thought about it, I remembered a friend of mine, a blind man who through faith saw the world clearly and changed thousands of lives.

Discussion Questions

1. What beliefs or teachings that you learned as a child have you adjusted as you matured in your faith?

2. What doubts have you wrestled with since becoming a Christian?

3. How have you benefited from studying the Bible?

4. What are some things we ought to keep in mind about God's Word as we study it?

2

"Just Have Faith"

Rediscovering Truth about Faith

He called me JJ, a nickname I earned doing something really embarrassing that I'd rather not go into right now. I called him B. By the time I met Brent Noebel—the son of Summit Ministries' founder, David Noebel—he had been struck with blindness and was losing his battle with diabetes.

Brent's blindness didn't stop him from doing much. He threw a football and flirted with girls, and we went to movies and listened to music and talked for hours. But when he realized that his life was coming to an end, Brent got on fire.

"JJ, I don't know how much time I have," he said. "But however long it is, I will make the biggest difference I can for God."

Every summer morning in Colorado, Brent and his seeing-eye dog, Bjorn, plodded over to the Summit Ministries classroom. He would lead students in the Pledge of Allegiance and then have all of them clear their throats before guiding them in the first verse of "Amazing Grace." Sing it through in your head and you'll know immediately why it was so important to Brent: "I once was lost, but now am found, was blind, but now I see."

Of all Brent's infirmities, the dark world of blindness had been the hardest to bear. He once told me, "I can handle just about anything, but the darkness of the last twenty years has been sheer torture."

Once when he was deathly ill, Brent received a telephone call from the amazing Joni Eareckson Tada, a woman who had become a quadriplegic through a diving accident at age seventeen. They talked about eternity:

"Brent, what are you going to do when you get to heaven?" she asked.

"I'm not sure what you mean," Brent replied.

"Well," Joni said, "*I* am going to *dance*."

"Oh, that sounds fantastic," Brent responded. "And *I* am going to *watch*."

Brent was eager for heaven. He was so tired. Not only of the darkness but also of the miserable effects of kidney disease and its treatment: despair, muscle cramps, sleeplessness. And the nonstop itchiness.

To rise above the misery, Brent became eager to invite as many people as possible to heaven. Whenever Brent met a stranger, he would discreetly produce a small handful of tracts, holding them down low between us as if he were asking advice about a gin rummy hand.

"JJ," he would whisper, "give me the one that ..."

I would curl his fingers around the one he was thinking of, and he would turn to the person with a smile. "Here's a short story about Jesus that has been very important to me. It will take only a few minutes to read. Will you promise to do it?"

"Why, thank you," the person would reply with a look of puzzled gratefulness. "I promise I will."

Once as we turned to leave, I said, "B, I have never seen a single person turn you down."

Brent replied with a chuckle, "What can I say, JJ? When you've got it, you've *got* it. People just can't say no to a blind guy."

Occasionally someone would thank Brent for maintaining a strong faith through so many trials. I could see it made him uncomfortable. He would fidget distractedly and change the subject as soon as it wasn't rude to do so.

The truth is, Brent didn't see his faith as being that strong. He was keenly aware of his shortcomings. He was weary of life. Conversations with Brent carried a sense of restlessness that I didn't understand until years later. People who know that any day could be their last will tell you it changes your perspective about everything. You feel anticipation that soon all things will be made new but also a growing sense of urgency about things left undone.

I experienced this duality once when frantically preparing for a speaking trip to Southeast Asia. I received a call from the airline to tell me the flight had been delayed by three hours. My first thought was

Good. Now I have time to finish some things. But my second thought was *Three hours? Come on. Let's get this show on the road!* I was still *in* my world of checking things off my to-do list, but I was no longer *of* it. My attitude became more intentional but also more impatient.

That sense of being *in* but not *of* characterized Brent's faith. He was confident that God was real and that his Word was true. He longed to be set free from his infirmities. But like the struggling yet determined test-taker when the proctor announces, "Five minutes," Brent felt an adrenaline surge to check his actions and motives, wanting to be found faithful (1 Cor. 4:2).

Four years before he died, Brent met a missionary who was delivering Bibles and medical supplies to Christians in southern Sudan. While enduring the dreary rigor of having all his blood removed and cleaned for four hours at a time, three days a week, Brent led the Summit Ministries students to raise nearly $300,000 for Sudanese Christians. When asked about this feat, Brent shrugged it off: "It just shows what one blind guy and a bunch of teenagers can do." Brent's faith combined firm knowledge with an urgency to live differently. Such faith bears little resemblance to the casual way Christians often treat discussions of faith. "Just have faith," we say, meaning "Hang in there." Yet the Bible doesn't tell us to "just have faith." It tells us to *live out* our faith. Biblical faith isn't believing something so strongly that it moves from being untrue to being true. Biblical faith is not merely about the power of belief (though beliefs certainly have the power to harm or help us). Rather, biblical faith is a kind of knowledge that is worth acting on with eyes wide open, because it is based on good reasons. So how did our understanding of faith get off track?

Where Did This Unquestioned Answer Come From?

"Faith is the opposite of logic," says an article on a popular Christian site.[1] If the author meant to say that faith is *illogical*, I heartily disagree. But I think I can see what the author meant. The Bible is full of accounts that defy natural explanation, from the parting of the Red Sea (Ex. 14:15–29) to the feeding of five thousand people with only five loaves and two fish (John 6:1–14). The Bible follows a deeper logic than people can attain if they cling to the belief that only the natural world exists.

The world mocks this way of expressing faith as a kind of blissful ignorance. Mark Twain sarcastically defined *faith* as "believing what you know ain't so."[2] Harvard professor Steven Pinker described faith as "believing something without good reasons to do so."[3] And the famous atheist Richard Dawkins said, "Faith is the great cop-out, the great excuse to evade the need to think and evaluate evidence. Faith is belief in spite of, even perhaps because of, the lack of evidence."[4]

But Twain, Pinker, and Dawkins have it exactly wrong. Everyone places faith in something. The question is whether the object of our faith is worthy. Biblically, faith isn't believing things that don't match up to reality. It's admitting that God *is* the greatest reality in the universe and then living as if that proposition is true. His revelation about himself solves the mysteries of knowledge and existence, bringing healing and purpose to our lives.

Even those who deny the power of faith still have it. My professors—I had more than seventy in college—were nearly all philosophical naturalists. They may not have been atheists per se, but they taught as if questions about God were irrelevant to their academic pursuits.

Occasionally this came up in class, though such discussions made me increasingly nervous as I moved closer to earning my PhD. In many doctoral programs, a professor's "thumbs-down" can get you kicked out without recourse.

One day, in the middle of a discussion about peace negotiations, a classmate of mine erupted, "We wouldn't have war if it weren't for Christians."

I couldn't believe it. "Excuse me?"

"It's true," he continued. "Think back on history. The Crusades. The Spanish Inquisition. This world will know peace only when people stop obsessing about God."

"You must have forgotten about the slaughter caused by *atheistic* leaders like Stalin, Pol Pot, and Mao," I snapped. "Their regimes killed more people than all the other wars in human history combined. You're getting faith and facts all mixed up."

Suddenly the professor interrupted: "Some people make their decisions by faith. Others make their decisions based on facts."

We all stopped and stared at him, trying to figure out why he had just said that. I broke the silence. "Carl," I asked—we called our professors by their first names in those days—"aren't there things you also believe by faith?"

I could immediately see that my question hit a nerve. He said, "You know, you're right. There are things I believe that I can't prove. I guess everyone has faith."

Carl was already my favorite professor. I liked him even more after that exchange. He could see that the "faith versus facts" framing wasn't really helpful in our mutual quest to grasp reality. The truth is, we all need a degree of faith to live. Even Richard Dawkins, the professor who called faith a cop-out, is a man of faith. He has faith in the laws of nature, such as the law of gravity, and doesn't worry about the potential existence of antigravity pockets by which people would be randomly flung into outer space. He has faith that his life is meaningful beyond evolutionary survival and that it should not be taken from him by someone whose chances of survival might increase by his death. On what is his faith based? If there is no designer behind the universe, what right do we have to expect that order rather than chaos will reign?

We are all people of faith—you and I and everyone else. Two questions face us: Are we justified in asserting that the beliefs in which we place our faith are true? If so, are we prepared to live as if they are true?

What the Bible Means by Faith

As I examined the topic of faith in the Bible, I realized that Scripture rarely encourages us to have faith. In fact, I can find only one instance where Jesus commands us to "have faith" (Mark 11:22). In that instance, though, his command refers to having faith *from* God.[5] What counts most is not the bigness of your belief but the bigness of the God who is there.

Years ago, I went rappelling for the first time. Rappelling is how climbers get down after ascending a rock face. They establish firm anchors for their rope, lean back into space, and descend toward the ground. Looking over the edge at the twelve-story drop, I was terrified. My guide calmly explained the strength of the rope, showed me the anchors he had carefully placed in the rock, and pointed out how my harness and rig were configured to protect me from a fall. As I stood shaking on the edge of the cliff, he asked, "Do you believe this rope is able to hold your weight?"

"Yes," I said, remembering what he had explained. "It could hold ten of me."

"Actually, far more than that, but good." He then asked, "Do you believe the anchors are well placed?"

"I do. I watched you set them. Each one by itself would be enough, and there are three."

"Good," he affirmed. "And do you believe your harness and rig are more than enough to keep you safe?"

"Yep," I said, looking him in the eye.

"If you believe all that, then *lean back*," he said, as if it were the simplest thing in the world.

I swallowed hard. Did I *really* believe? If so, action would naturally follow. Silently I confessed several sins that came to mind. I took a deep breath and leaned away from the edge of the cliff, out beyond where I could avoid a death plunge if something went wrong. The rope held as I bounced my way down the wall with childlike glee.

On that rock face, my faith wasn't based on wishful thinking. It was based on knowledge of the equipment and safety procedures. In a similar way, biblical faith is firm knowledge of reality, based on the most trustworthy source in the universe. Action flows naturally from faith. You know you are faithful when your everyday actions prove what you say you believe. This is not to say that our works save us, but it is to say that *faith works*. James 2:18 says, "Someone will say, 'You have faith and I have works.' Show me your faith apart from your works, and I will show you my faith by my works." Faith is both "show" and "tell."

As we saw in the previous chapter, the Bible encourages believers to have good reasons for what they believe. For his gospel, Luke—a medical doctor—interviewed eyewitnesses and carefully investigated the disciples' claims "so that you may know the exact truth about the things you have been taught" (1:4 NASB). Knowledge led to truth. Truth led to confidence. Confidence bolstered faith.

At the same time, the Bible proclaims a deeper reality beyond knowledge of the natural world. This kind of spiritual wisdom enables us to "walk in a manner worthy of the Lord, fully pleasing to him: bearing fruit in every good work and increasing in the knowledge of God" (Col. 1:10).

It's beneficial to understand the Greek word for "faith," which is used hundreds of times in the Gospels and the letters of the apostles. The word for "faith" is *pistis*, the same word that Greek philosophers such as Aristotle used to describe the unstated premise, or basis, of an argument. Faith is the basis of life in the same way that mathematical reasoning is the basis of knowing that two plus two equals four or that sense perception is the basis of knowing that a pan just pulled from the oven is too hot to touch. Our faith in mathematical reasoning and sense perception is deeply ingrained. We don't bother trying to explain them. They are *pistis*.

We take far more for granted than we realize. For instance, some time ago twelve young soccer players and their twentysomething coach found themselves trapped in a cave in Thailand. Rising water from heavy rainstorms stranded the group so far from the entrance that reaching them required a perilous six-hour journey of scuba diving and underground hiking. It was a miracle that they were even found.

The rescue operation took more than two weeks and involved more than a hundred divers, a hundred government agencies, hundreds of police officers, and thousands of soldiers and volunteers. The world was transfixed by the drama of the rescue. A Google search of "Tham Luang cave rescue" yielded nearly three hundred thousand hits. I didn't read all the articles, of course, but I did go several pages deep into the search results. Most of the articles were about how the rescue was going or about strategies that rescuers might employ. Not one article asked "Why?" *No one* questioned whether the extreme risk and vast amount of effort were worth it. The belief that human life is valuable is properly basic to our thinking. It is something we don't even bother to contemplate in such a situation. It is *pistis*.

The writers of the New Testament used the Greek word *pistis* for "faith" because to their way of thinking, faith is the unstated premise of life itself. God has told us what is true. We trust him. We're moving into action. Faith is the basis of life. Without it nothing makes sense.

The Bible treats faith as knowledge about God that we are justified in having. We can know things and we can act on what we know. Through Jesus we can know God, be known by him, and know how to live in the world around us.

Importantly, we don't need to be 100 percent certain about something for it to count as knowledge. As philosopher J. P. Moreland pointed out, believing in God isn't the same as being free of all doubt. You can trust in God, believe he speaks through the Bible, trust that he rose from the dead—and admit that you don't have the answer to every question.[6] Ironically faith can be made stronger *through* doubt. As Pastor Timothy Keller put it, "A faith without some doubts is like a human body without any antibodies in it."[7] A faith with some doubts can still be a strong faith as long as we are willing to act on it.

If you wait around until you know everything and are free from doubt, you'll never join a church or fall in love or, for that matter, drive a car or make a friend. Faith is not about being absolutely sure. It's about holding rational beliefs and acting on what you know so far, allowing God to guide you (Ps. 119:105; Prov. 3:5–6).

What Must We Do Now?

Nearly two thousand years ago, a man named Mathetes (mahth-ee-TEESE) sat quietly in a darkened room, listening to soft conversations echoing off the stone walls. He found himself in a new type of religious gathering. The service had started off fairly typically, as religious services go. Scriptures had been read and prayers offered. But what Mathetes found so unusual was the complete lack of ecstasy or mindlessness that was typical at the time. Indeed, the service seemed to focus on the participants thinking aloud about the teaching, asking questions, and listening. They weren't learning the universe's secrets. They were learning how to *live*.

Though he had been attending meetings for some time now and had even led others to faith, it struck Mathetes afresh how completely unlike Roman religious ceremonies this was. His friends called these people "atheists" because they rejected the pantheon of Roman gods and instead insisted that the one true God made everything and welcomed humanity into a personal relationship through his Son, *Christos*. Mathetes realized now that these people weren't atheists. They were living out a faith so profound that Rome, with all its history, all its philosophy, and all its power, could do nothing to stop it.

After slipping quietly out of the gathering, Mathetes wandered the smoke- and sewage-choked streets until he arrived at his humble dwelling. There he took an ember from the community fire, fanned his small lamp into flame, and began to write on a piece of parchment, "Most Excellent Diognetus ..."

Mathetes's letter to Diognetus is now considered the earliest surviving defense for the Christian faith. Mathetes—his name is a generic word for "disciple"—wrote this about Christians: "They love all men, and are persecuted by all.... They are dishonoured, and yet in their very dishonour are glorified."[8]

When Christianity first began to spread, Rome was a haughty and aristocratic culture with no respect for ordinary people. Based on Jesus's teaching that the last will be first and the first will be last (Matt. 20:16; Mark 10:43; Luke 22:27), early Christians elevated the status of women, cared for the sick, and took in the poor.

Christians met physical needs without sacrificing faith in a future hope. It was an entirely new way to live, and it spread like wildfire. Why? In their book *The Unshakable Truth*, Josh McDowell and Sean McDowell say that it's because the early church focused on three disciplines: *believing, belonging,* and *behaving.* The early church's resulting level of growth was unprecedented in the history of religion. The McDowells quote sources who say the number of Christians in the early church grew from twenty-five thousand to twenty million believers in just two hundred years.[9]

Throughout history the teachings of Christ have affected countless cultures. Sadly, some have used Jesus's teachings for personal gain or tried to spread Jesus's gospel in ways Jesus himself condemned. Yet at various times, Christians living changed lives in light of their faith altered the course of civilization. Here are two quirky examples.

Celtic Christianity of the fifth through ninth centuries spread through monks who went on pilgrimages, sometimes launching themselves in animal-skin boats without oars or sails, believing God would guide them to where he wanted them to spread his good news. In the 500s an Irish monk named Columbanus embarked on a lifelong pilgrimage. He traveled to Britain and then France and ultimately overland to Switzerland and Italy. Along the way he established monasteries to promote literacy and learning so people could better know God. Many of these monasteries became celebrated institutions of education, even sending out missionaries of their own.[10] Some monastic schools eventually developed into universities. In this strange way the faith of the Irish saved civilization.

Once universities were established, the advance of science and technology became inevitable. Beginning in the twelfth century, scientists who believed in a divine Creator began systematizing their knowledge about the world. The unfortunately named Robert Grosseteste (his last name may be translated "fat head") developed methods for observing and experimenting with nature.[11] You've probably never heard of Professor Fat Head (c. 1170–1253), but you've almost certainly heard of Roger Bacon (c. 1220–1292), one of his Oxford students, who applied Grosseteste's methods to a range of fields, laying the foundation for the Scientific Revolution.[12]

It was here that Columbanus and Grosseteste demonstrated the kind of faith we're describing. They believed by faith, cultivated knowledge through faith, and acted as if their faith were true. The world could not help but be changed as a result.

Both men would fit well in the "faith chapter" of Hebrews 11, where we read, "By faith we understand that the universe was created by the word of God, so that what is seen was not made out of things that are visible" (v. 3). Hebrews 11 is the starting lineup of the faithful: Abel, Enoch, Abraham, Sarah, Moses, Rahab, and on and on. After this retelling, the author concluded, "Therefore, since we are surrounded by so great a cloud of witnesses, let us also lay aside every weight, and sin which clings so closely, and let us run with endurance the race that is set before us, looking to Jesus, the founder and perfecter of our faith, who for the joy that was set before him endured the cross, despising the shame, and is seated at the right hand of the throne of God" (12:1–2).

Faithfulness is like a relay race that has gone on for thousands of years, and now it's our turn. Here comes the runner, baton in hand, calling out, "Are you ready?"

What will the story of our time be? Will we continue to say things like "Just have faith" and treat faith as if believing in something unreal will make it real? Or will we realize faith is a gift from God that is the basis for all of life?

———

The last time I saw Brent, he was hosting an auction with the Summit staff to raise funds for Sudan. It was a Wednesday evening. On

Thursday morning Brent led the students in the Pledge of Allegiance and "Amazing Grace." He went off to the dialysis clinic, and shortly afterward, I stood up to give my presentation to the students. Afterward I caught a flight back home to Tennessee. When my plane landed, I received word that Brent had passed away.

Through my tears I imagined how surprised Brent must have been. The pinch of the dialysis port … the nurse helping him with his headphones … drifting off to sleep for the four-hour procedure … and then waking up in heaven. I wondered what that was like for Brent to have suffered the horror of utter blackness for twenty years and then open his eyes to see Jesus's face.

Even though Brent has been gone for nearly two decades, you'll still notice his touch if you attend a Summit Ministries program. Each morning students begin with the Pledge of Allegiance. Then they pause, clear their throats just as Brent did, and sing,

> Amazing grace! how sweet the sound,
> That saved a wretch; like me!
> I once was lost, but now am found,
> Was blind, but now I see.[13]

It's not a memorial to Brent but a daily reminder to live by faith until we know what Brent now knows with crystal clarity: biblical faith isn't blind. It's an eyes-wide-open trust in a God who is there and who is worthy.

Yet even for those who live lives of faith, another question arises: How do we connect with this God we know to be real? Do we plug into him like a wall socket? Do we perform incantations to get his attention? Even longtime Christians get confused. It's too bad, because what God tells us about how to communicate with him and what he insists that we ask him for are almost beyond belief.

Discussion Questions

1. How is the notion of faith often misunderstood by Christians and non-Christians alike?

2. Did this chapter challenge any of your beliefs about biblical faith? How?

3. What do you think it means to live faithfully? In what do you place your faith?

4. How does living out what you believe show your faith to others?

3

"God Will Heal Our Land If We Humble Ourselves and Pray"

Rediscovering Truth about Prayer

A friend of mine visited a jewelry shop in London and asked the clerk, "Do you have cross necklaces?"

"Oh yes, we have plain ones, and we also have ones with a little man on them," said the eager clerk, seemingly unaware of who the "little man" was. And this was in England, a nation dominated by Christianity for a thousand years.

As civilizations prosper, they get lazy and cut themselves off from the principles that made them great. Cathedrals remain standing long after people have stopped worshipping in them. National monuments don't disintegrate just because citizens scorn the beliefs of those in whose honor they were built. Families experience this too. Research shows that up to 90 percent of affluent families lose their wealth by the third generation.[1] The first generation works, the second generation manages, and the third generation plays.

When it comes to living out faith, many parents can testify to the heartbreak they feel as they watch their children who once worshipped Jesus with abandon grow cold toward him. It's a distress known well in the time of the apostle Paul, who warned his protégé, Timothy, that in the last days people would be "lovers of pleasure rather than lovers of God, having the appearance of godliness, but denying its power" (2 Tim. 3:4–5).

As I pondered the difficulty of passing faith from one generation to the next, my planned chapter on prayer turned into something much more. It's a cautionary tale about treating prayer as a mystical incantation in which we implore God to do what he did for our ancestors, rather than as a powerful conversation with him about his kingdom being realized on earth as it is in heaven (Matt. 6:10).

At the heart of the discussion is what I consider to be one of Christianity's most beloved unquestioned answers, one that appears to be a rock-solid promise of revival and is often invoked publicly, such as in this "Power of Election Prayer":

Dear Heavenly Father, You have given us this promise: "If my people, who are called by my

name, will humble themselves and pray and
seek my face and turn from their wicked ways,
then will I hear from heaven and will forgive
their sin and will heal their land" (2 Chronicles
7:14). So, we pray to you. We turn from evil and
look to you, our God. Please: unite us, strengthen
us, appoint and anoint our next president. In
the name of Christ we pray, Amen.[2]

These words, based on 2 Chronicles 7:14, form a compelling call
to unite around God's promises for national healing and justice. People
I deeply respect and admire earnestly cite its beautiful words as a call
to national repentance. We may feel our nation's lack of spiritual focus
and fervently desire that God will heal our land. But does our sincere
use of the passage mean that it applies to us, or is it an unquestioned
answer that muddies the waters about how to properly interpret and
apply Scripture to our own lives, especially regarding vitally important
spiritual disciplines such as prayer? I tend toward the latter view. We
don't need to try to force God to keep a promise that was not made to
us. Scripture—especially the direct words of Jesus—shows us that the
God of the universe has invited us to ask and has promised to answer.
There's more hope in this than any formula could give.

Where Does This Unquestioned Answer Come From?

I believe in the power of prayer, though I haven't written much
about it. Several years ago, I penned three lengthy textbooks about

a biblical worldview. I recently reviewed what I said about prayer in those pages. I'm ashamed to say that I included only a handful of paragraphs about prayer in more than 1,500 pages.

By not drawing attention to the Bible's teachings on prayer, I missed much of what is important about Scripture. Prayer is central to the Bible. It is not a superficial act of self-talk. Through prayer we converse with God, letting go of the illusion that we are in control, lamenting our failings, and sharing our longings with the One who has our best interests at heart.

Through prayer God changes us so we see the world from his perspective. This may be why we find passages such as 2 Chronicles 7:14 so compelling. We realize our brokenness and our need for redemption.

In America, national calls to prayer and repentance are commonplace, even as fewer and fewer people claim belief in the God of the Bible. Especially in times of calamity, we turn to prayer. In a 1970 Independence Day ceremony at the Lincoln Memorial, evangelist Billy Graham put it beautifully: "We have stood tall in America in most areas, but on this Independence Day I call upon Americans to bend low before God and go to their knees as Washington and Lincoln called us to our knees many years ago. No nation is ever taller than when on its knees. I submit that we can best honor America by rededicating ourselves to God and the American dream."[3]

Christians believe that unless the church takes prayer and repentance seriously, our nation will never experience awakening. Talking about how the Jesus Revolution brought hope out of the turbulent 1960s, evangelist Greg Laurie said, "As believers, we want God to heal our land and change our nation for the better, but as we look at the problems in our country, it's sometimes easier to just point at someone else."[4]

I admire bold Christian leaders who long for revival. I consider myself to be a patriotic American who believes my country has been a powerful force for good in the world. And I try to be honest about my country's shortcomings and work to fix them.

Many people assume that because much good has been done—often by people whose actions were motivated by Jesus—God is somehow obligated to extend to us the promises he made to ancient Israel. But there are three reasons why this is misguided.

First, claiming that God will heal *our* land if we pray makes it seem as if our nation is specially chosen by God. In the 1951 book *Christ and Culture*, H. Richard Niebuhr referred to this as the "Christ of culture" viewpoint. It's the view held by some in our history who claimed that America was a new Israel. This perspective was apparently shared by rationalists such as Thomas Jefferson, who seemed to believe that the life of reason forms a uniquely good culture, on which Jesus would have certainly put his stamp of approval.[5] But what if Christ came to *transform* culture, not to put his stamp on any particular expression of it?

Second, it is a mistake to individualize the text by assuming that any or all parts of the Bible apply to us in a unique way outside their original context. Examples of individualizing the text are "David calmed Saul by playing his harp; therefore, it is important to have calming music in our services" and "Gideon put a fleece out to test God; therefore, it is good to test God so he can show himself faithful."

Third, we distort the Bible's teaching by misapplying what was originally intended. A common example is Matthew 18:19–20: "Again I say to you, if two of you agree on earth about anything they ask, it will be done for them by my Father in heaven. For where two or three are gathered in my name, there am I among them." This is often taken as a promise that God will grant whatever believers request when they get together to pray in the name of Jesus. But if you back up just a few verses, it is clear that Jesus was referring to having two or three witnesses present to help resolve a conflict. In fact, the phrase "two or three witnesses" (v. 16), while used several times in Scripture, is never used except in reference to the testimony of witnesses in establishing justice.[6] If we take it in context, we can easily see this verse is about resolving conflicts among believers and not about prayer.

In order to know what the Bible is telling us about the true power of prayer, we need to first learn how to properly understand and apply Scripture.

Understanding and Applying the Bible to Our Lives

I cringe thinking of all the times I've made mistakes in explaining Scripture and applying it to life, especially in public speeches. Because I know my Bible knowledge is lacking, I now run everything I'm thinking by trusted Bible scholars who help me properly interpret Scripture. Here are four steps I've learned from my mentors.

Step 1: Understand What You're Reading

Imagine you come across a last will and testament for sale for five dollars in an antique store. The document details the assets of a prominent woman who died many years ago, expressing her desire to leave her heirs one million dollars. Intrigued, you plunk down five dollars, drive downtown, and march into the attorney's office listed on the letterhead. You present the will and demand your share. Will you get it? Of course not. The will wasn't written for you.

This doesn't mean your five dollars was wasted. You can still learn a lot about how wills were written in the old days, the person who drafted the will, what assets she had, and why she divided them the way she did. It is a treasure trove of local history. But to claim the money for yourself is to misunderstand the document's intent.

Scripture contains many promises. God promised Abraham that he would be the father of a great nation (Gen. 12:2). God promised David that he would make his name great (2 Sam. 7:9). God promised Solomon that he would grant his request for wisdom and add to it immense wealth and power (1 Kings 3:12–13). We intuitively understand that while God's character is unchanging, these promises are not for us and we are not entitled to claim them as our own.

Yet there are also many promises in Scripture that apply to *any* reader. Knowing the difference takes two kinds of skill. The first skill is a large-scale understanding of how to interpret Scripture. The second skill requires focusing on detail and is the difficult but rewarding small-scale work of wrestling with each chapter, verse, line, and word. Applying these two skills helps us avoid inserting our own biases and cultural assumptions into the text.[7] Properly understanding Scripture takes both a general ability to interpret and a focus on detail.

Step 2: Understand the Context

The historical background and literary characteristics of a text, as well as the discourse surrounding a passage, give meaning to the content. To discern the historical context, ask questions such as these: When and where was it written? What was happening at the time culturally and politically? Who was the original audience? Why did the author write it? What motivated him, and what was he hoping to achieve?

Literary context refers to the genre, structure, and grammar of a text. What kind of writing is it? A psalm? A letter? A prophetic oracle? A historical narrative? Here's a question we should ask of every biblical book, passage, paragraph, and sentence: What is the main point the author is trying to get across?

For example, in Matthew 12, Jesus discussed the Pharisees' misunderstanding of the Sabbath. He said, "The Son of Man is lord of the Sabbath" (v. 8). To make sense of this, we need to read the end of the previous chapter: "Come to me, all who labor and are heavy laden, and I will give you rest" (11:28). *Jesus* is our Sabbath. He is our rest.

In Scripture everything is related to everything else. The smaller stories add up to one big story. Theologians call this the "metanarrative." As Michael Goheen put it, "The biblical story encompasses all of reality—north, south, east, west, past, present, and future."[8]

Step 3: Understand What the Passage Says about God

If the Bible is a story about everything and it is God's story, then in addition to the historical and literary context, we need to ask, What does this say about God? We need to understand what God is like and what he wants to happen in the world. Going back to 2 Chronicles 7:14, we cannot assume that God will act toward our nation as he acted toward Israel. He hasn't made us that promise. We can say, however, that this passage reveals some aspects of God's character that have always been true—such as God's desire for relationship, his honoring of the humble, his desire for us to pray, and his hope that we turn from wickedness. If we stop trying to claim promises that may not belong to us, we will be free to focus on God and his plans rather than on whether our nation is failing to receive blessings.

To approach the text well, we need to ask questions like these:

- What does God reveal about himself?
- What does God care about?
- What does God tell us about his plans?
- What does God want us to be like?
- What kind of communication does God want with us?

Asking these questions opens a window into God's unchanging nature so we better understand how to more fully bear his image.

Step 4: Understand What the Passage Calls You to Do

Scripture passages are usually either descriptive or prescriptive. From descriptive passages, we see what life was like in ancient times. We learn how God's people failed and what God called them to do to find restoration. These passages give us tremendous insight into what God is like and what is important to him. But these passages are merely describing what happened, not telling us what to do. These are some examples:

- Abraham taking his son Isaac to Mount Moriah to offer him as a sacrifice (Gen. 22:1–14)
- Ruth getting Boaz's attention so he will marry her (Ruth 3:6–13)
- early church members giving away their possessions and living communally (Acts 2:44–47)
- Paul getting bitten by a poisonous snake and surviving (Acts 28:3–5)

Other passages are prescriptive, which means they provide specific guidance for how we ought to live, make decisions, and think. Many prescriptive passages reflect something of God's nature and his created order. These passages are essentially commands to be obeyed or values to be adopted. These include the following:

- the Ten Commandments (Ex. 20:2–17)
- the Sermon on the Mount (Matt. 5:2—7:27)
- the Great Commission (Matt. 28:18–20)

We learn from both descriptive passages and prescriptive ones, but prescriptive passages are particularly useful for our growth as believers. People may choose to "lay out fleeces" to determine God's will, as Gideon did, or play harps to soothe angry bosses or drink wine when their stomachs are upset, but they shouldn't tell others that the Bible told them to do so.

What Must We Do Now?

Let's return to 2 Chronicles 7:14, the passage at the heart of this chapter's unquestioned answer. Using the criteria just discussed, it seems this is a descriptive passage revealing how God dealt with the nation of Israel. Yet Scripture provides many prescriptive passages about prayer, which we can learn from and apply.

First, Scripture calls for us to pray with confidence. Ephesians 3:12 says we have "boldness and access with confidence through our faith in him." Hebrews calls us to "with confidence draw near to the throne of grace" (4:16) and to "draw near with a true heart in full assurance of faith" (10:22). The apostle John said, "This is the confidence that we have toward him, that if we ask anything according to his will he hears us. And if we know that he hears us in whatever we ask, we know that we have the requests that we have asked of him" (1 John 5:14–15).

Second, Scripture calls for us to pray faithfully and continually (Luke 11:5–13; 18:1–8; 1 Thess. 5:17). The apostle Paul said, "Rejoice in hope, be patient in tribulation, be constant in prayer" (Rom. 12:12) and "Do not be anxious about anything, but in everything by prayer and supplication with thanksgiving let your requests be made known to God" (Phil. 4:6). Also, "Continue steadfastly in prayer, being watchful in it with thanksgiving" (Col. 4:2).

Third, even when we feel that he is not hearing us, Scripture calls us to pray in faith that God will respond. John 15:7 tells us, "If you abide in me, and my words abide in you, ask whatever you wish, and it will be done for you." And according to Matthew, "Ask, and it will be given to you; seek, and you will find; knock, and it will be opened to you. For everyone who asks receives, and the one who seeks finds, and to the one who knocks it will be opened" (7:7–8).

Scripture's clear commands about prayer—and their attached promises—call for us to do two things.

Reject Functional Atheism

I admit that when I have prayed publicly, my prayers have often been vague and cowardly. On reflection I think I was hesitant because, well, what if God didn't answer my request? I didn't want others to be disappointed in him or doubt him. Deep in my heart, though, was a self-centered focus. I didn't want to face embarrassment myself.

I'm not alone in being hesitant about prayer. Like many, I grew up in a secular culture in which it was fine to believe in God as long as you didn't take your belief too seriously. For much of my life, I was functionally an atheist—I believed in God but acted as if he were irrelevant to what was important. Fortunately, I've had lots of encouragement in rethinking my assumptions.[9] Some of that rethinking resulted from prayer time with my own children. One evening my young son said, "Papa, I'm afraid to go to sleep because I'll have nightmares."

"Would you like me to pray with you?"

"Yeah."

"God," I said, using my best prayer voice, "help my son to have good dreams tonight. Help him to dream about nice things. Puppies. Kittens. Birds—"

His eyes flew open. "Birds aren't nice," he accused.

All at once I was struck with conviction. I wasn't praying to God. I was trying to psych my son into having nice dreams.

"I've been praying all wrong," I said. "Can I start over?"

He nodded.

"God, I pray that you would make my son into a brave warrior for you. Make him fierce against anything that is wrong and unjust. Give him courage to face his fears knowing that you guard him with your mighty hand. Through your mercy and strength, prepare my son to be kind, a man who always looks out for the little guy. We know you answer prayer, and we send him off to bed with confidence tonight. In Jesus's powerful name, amen."

My son slept in peace. Moreover, in the years since, he has become a fierce protector of those who are vulnerable. In his school he's known as a trusted friend of the little guy. A brave warrior indeed. I'm convinced that bold prayer played a role in setting him on that course.

Embrace Prayer's True Power

If I'm honest, I sometimes wonder whether Jesus's commands about prayer—and his promises to answer—might be a little too good to be true. I've heard "name it and claim it" preachers say that we should demand that God meet our materialistic desires. One such preacher called on his followers to believe God for a brand-new Falcon 7X, a $54 million private jet (for him, not for them).[10] This is a tough ask in a world where seven hundred million people live on less than two dollars a day.[11]

Obviously, asking God for a luxury jet is an extreme example. Yet such examples shouldn't dissuade us from praying as God encourages us to do. As one Christian philosopher put it, "Why should I forgo the tremendous blessings of fruit bearing that Jesus promised because some woefully imprudent ministers want to make it all about them and their lavish lifestyle? Not a chance."[12]

So what should we pray for? We can pray boldly and with certainty that

- God's kingdom will come and his will be done on earth as it is in heaven (Matt. 6:10);
- God will forgive our sins (1 John 1:9);
- God's presence will be with us (Isa. 58:9);
- we will have wisdom (James 1:5);
- the Lord will be a stronghold for the oppressed (Ps. 9:9);
- God will meet all our needs (Phil. 4:19);
- the sick will be healed (James 5:14–15);
- we will be given everything we need to bear fruit for him (John 15:16).

And these are just for starters. If you don't believe me, just start looking up Bible passages about prayer. You may be stunned, as I was, at how generous God really is.

The truth is, we don't need to recite and pray 2 Chronicles 7:14 in order for God to fulfill his promises. Instead, God wants us to boldly align our wills with his, praying that what is important to him will be recognized as what's important here on earth.

When I became president of Summit Ministries, the ministry was facing difficult decisions. The financial and ministry trends were downward. As I struggled for a message to encourage our dedicated staff, I settled on two things.

First, we must pray and be willing to act on what God leads us to do. Prayer doesn't replace action; it sparks it. When Nehemiah returned from captivity to rebuild Jerusalem's broken walls, he reminded the people of Israel, "Remember the Lord, who is great and awesome, and fight for your brothers, your sons, your daughters, your wives, and your homes" (Neh. 4:14). Couched in the middle of a descriptive passage is a prescription about how to act wisely, recognizing that God is who he says he is.

Second, we must pray expecting God to move in the ways he has promised, not expecting that he will make things easier. After teaching his disciples about the power of prayer, Jesus said, "In the world you will have tribulation. But take heart; I have overcome the world" (John 16:33). Military generals don't long for opportunities to avoid the enemy. Rather, they request the equipment and person-nel needed to obtain victory. Prayer is the same for us. God wants to give us everything we need to accomplish what he asks of us.

Take a close look at both of those points. They're not about "me"; they're about "we." Often we think of prayer as an individual pursuit. And while times of solitary prayer are powerful, we are not meant to be lone rangers. This is important to keep in mind as we move into the next chapter on Christian community. "Me and Jesus" may make a good foot-tapping country song, but it leads us into a spiritual desert at the very moment God invites us to join his feast.

Discussion Questions

1. Have you ever been angry at God because you thought he promised you something but never delivered?

2. Why is context important when reading the Bible? How can you keep from taking God's words out of context?

3. What role does prayer play in your life?

4. What steps would you like to take to strengthen your prayer life?

4

"It's Just Me and Jesus"

Rediscovering Truth about Community

On May 2, 2013, country music superstar Brad Paisley stepped to the microphone in front of an audience of other country superstars and crooned, "Me and Jesus got our own thing going; / We don't need anybody to tell us what it's all about."[1]

The event was the memorial service of another country music legend, George Jones, who had sung "Me and Jesus" as an anthem of defiance in the middle of what turned out to be a decades-long battle with alcoholism. Nicknamed "No Show Jones" for his many canceled appearances, Jones seems to have been saying, "You don't understand me, but Jesus does. I have him, so I don't need you."

"Me and Jesus" sums up the attitude many self-professed Christians today have toward church. "My faith is my own," they say. "I don't need a church. It's just me and Jesus." Some people think they can "do church" by listening to a podcast or having a Bible reading at home with their families. Others gather with friends, and if the conversation turns to God, they consider that to be church. Others say "Nature is my church" and just go boating.

You might assume that people who don't attend church stay away because they don't believe what is taught there. But that's not the main reason, according to research from the Pew organization: only 28 percent of nonattenders said they don't attend church because they are not believers. According to the report, "More say they practice their faith in other ways (37%) or they haven't found a church or other house of worship that they like (23%). About 1 in 5 say they don't like the sermons (18%) or cite logistical problems (22%)."[2]

Increasingly, people don't feel they need church. According to Barna Group, such people "still love Jesus, still believe in Scripture and most of the tenets of their Christian faith. But they have lost faith in the church."[3]

They may have a point. All week we put up with inconveniences. Then on our one free day we're asked to gather with people we don't know, in a place we don't feel comfortable, at a time dictated by others, to hear something we've already heard from people we aren't sure we trust … after which all of us go about our lives as if nothing significant happened. Might as well just go for a hike.

But what if the "just me and Jesus" trend keeps us from experiencing true power, blessing, purpose, and growth? What if there's something about church that isn't just another thing to do each week but is at the center of the meaningful lives God intends us to have?

Where Does This Unquestioned Answer Come From?

A growing number of people see their faith as a private concern and don't feel a need to attend church in order to express it.[4] At Summit Ministries we've watched this trend with growing alarm, especially as it affects young adults. As I mentioned in the introduction, two-thirds of young adults who regularly attended church for at least a year as teenagers are no longer attending church as twentysomethings. About a third of those will eventually return and attend church regularly, but most just leave and never look back.[5]

When speaking about young adults' abandonment of church, I sometimes ask the audience to imagine a student named Dalton. He grew up in church and felt at home in the company of people with sincerely held beliefs. He looked forward to being able to take on his college professors with the clever repartees the pastor shared from the pulpit.

Then Dalton arrived at his history of civilizations class to find that his professor was charming and genuinely helpful, a contrast to the "angry atheist" stereotype he was led to expect. Even though the professor taught that the Bible was filled with myths, he showed sensitivity to the feelings of believers and illustrated each point with compelling examples.

At the end of class each day, Dalton returned to his residence hall, where no one prayed, talked about Jesus, or attended church, and they didn't seem to feel guilty about it. Gradually Dalton let down his guard and started adopting the lifestyle of those around him. He knew that people from his home church would be horrified if they discovered that he went out drinking and that his girlfriend sometimes spent the night in his dorm room. His conscience bothered him, but staying busy and avoiding church kept the tension at bay. *Besides,* he told himself, *I'm an adult now, and I can make my own decisions.*

Dalton is a composite of young adults I've worked with over the years. But Dalton is also me. As a college student, my spiritual weakness kept me from church, and staying away from church increased my spiritual weakness.

It's easy to blame colleges and universities for stripping the faith of young people, but that doesn't tell the whole story. Sociologists reported that those who don't attend college after high school are even more likely than college-goers to curb their church attendance.[6] Something deeper is going on. Fortunately, new insight from Fuller Youth Institute shows that faith drift is not inevitable. Researchers followed over five hundred youth group graduates in their first three years of college. They found that churches characterized by these four things help students stay strong in their faith:

- intergenerational relationships (being surrounded by at least five caring adults)
- whole gospel (integrating faith into every area of life)
- partnership with families (parent involvement)

- being a safe place for doubt ("Doubt is
  not toxic to faith; silence is," researchers
  concluded)[7]

Fuller's research demonstrates that the most spiritually connected young people are those whose churches have become a significant plotline in the story of their lives. This result is consistent with other research correlating church attendance with a good life. People today are lonelier than ever before, which is related to all sorts of physical and emotional problems. Churchgoers suffer far less than others because they're involved in communities where they are part of something bigger than themselves. People who regularly attend worship services are more likely to donate money and time and help others.[8] People who believe their spiritual lives are about "just me and Jesus," rather than being part of a church, miss out. These people need you. And you need them.

What Is Church?

If you ask people to define church, they often define it by what people *do* in a church building—listen to teaching, sing, visit with friends. The biblical idea of church is much richer. In Old Testament times, people connected to God with the help of priests as they offered sacrifices for their sins or out of thankfulness for God's generosity. In the light of Jesus's death and resurrection, a clearer picture emerged: we too are priests! The apostle Peter wrote, "You are a chosen race, a royal priesthood, a holy nation, a people for his own possession, that you may proclaim the excellencies of him who called you out of darkness into his marvelous light. Once you were not a people, but now you are God's people; once you had not received mercy, but now you have received mercy" (1 Pet. 2:9–10).

We can't just turn our spiritual development over to priests. We *are* priests! We don't go to church merely to connect with God; we go to learn how to connect *others* with God. Going to church just to be ministered to is like going to cooking school to learn to eat. It misses the whole point.

In the New Testament, the word for "church" is *ekklēsia*, a community united by God's Spirit and charged with proclaiming the reality of Christ's kingdom to the whole world. Made up of both Jews and non-Jews (Gentiles), the church was a new kind of community that helped people become a "new creation" (2 Cor. 5:17).

Very simply, the church today is called to spread the good news about God, just as Israel had been instructed to do (Isa. 49:6; Matt. 28:18–20). It is through the church that God is working his plan to redeem his people. The church is a central character in the story of God, a story that encompasses every day of our lives.

Yet there is a difference between the way we use the term *church* in referring to God's plan for his people and the way we more commonly use *church* to mean the physical place we gather each week. Is it possible to be a part of *the* church without being committed to *a* church? The apostles didn't offer that option. Hebrews 10:23–25 says, "Let us hold fast the confession of our hope without wavering, for he who promised is faithful. And let us consider how to stir up one another to love and good works, not neglecting to meet together, as is the habit of some, but encouraging one another, and all the more as you see the Day drawing near."

This "gathering together" is described in detail in the New Testament: what the leaders should do, how we should behave when we are together, what to think about and pray for, and how to live out our faith in daily life.

Why Do We Need Church?

The apostles used many familiar metaphors to help people see what this new thing—the church—was all about. They described it as the bride of Jesus (Eph. 5:25–32). It's an army equipped to support good and fight against the forces of spiritual destruction (Eph. 6:10–18). It's a body made up of parts that interconnect and rely on one another (1 Cor. 12:12–27). It's a family (Eph. 2:19).

Church is a regular invitation to proclaim truth through worship, and church is how we grow spiritually. It is where we can be restored in relationship with the one true God and where we learn to serve for all the right reasons. Church restores our hope. Let's look at each of these in turn.

Proclaiming God's Truth through Worship

Worship leader Matt Redman said true worshippers "gather beneath the shadow of the Cross, where an undying devotion took the Son of God to His death. Alive now in the power of His resurrection, they respond to such an outpouring with an unquenchable offering of their own."[9]

Worshipping together with other believers ought to be like a family reunion. Of course, reunions are painful for some families, but it is up to each person to bring healing. When you don't feel like worshipping, often the joy or intensity of someone else's worship can be contagious. It restores you in a way that singing in the shower never can.

Another aspect of worship is Communion, which should never be treated as just another ritual. Theologian Alexander Schmemann said, "The liturgy of [Communion] is best understood as a journey or procession. It is the journey of the Church into the dimension of the Kingdom."[10]

Growing Spiritually Together

Spiritual growth happens best in community. God never intended for humans to grow up spiritually alone. The apostles speak frequently of spiritual growth in their letters, almost all of which were written to groups of people, not individuals. Spiritual growth is not a "me and Jesus" thing. It's an all-of-us-together thing through which God enables good things to flow into our lives. As author and teacher Parker Palmer put it, "Community doesn't just create abundance—community *is* abundance."[11]

We experience the best of God's abundance in our "withness," our being *with* others. Obviously, this kind of community calls for deeper engagement than just getting together with cherished friends over cups of coffee. A dominant metaphor for the church in the New Testament is that of a body (Rom. 12:4–5; 1 Cor. 12:12–27). The strength the arm needs to perform wasn't given to the arm alone.

It was given to the circulatory system, the nervous system, and the brain's coordinating function. If you see an arm all by itself, something very bad has happened.

Being Restored

The body of Christ is a shield that protects us from our own inclinations, the temptations of the world, and spiritual forces of darkness.

Some churches use tearful altar calls to urge people to repent. Those who feel emotionally touched respond, while those who are not emotionally touched do not. But repentance isn't about whether we "feel it." Repentance is to the soul what nutrition is to the body. You don't wait to eat until you feel as if you are dying; you eat regularly so you never get to that place.

Repentance involves soul-searching. Is there rebellion in your heart? Are you hiding from God's presence in any area of life? Have you acted toward your neighbor in a way that was ungodly? Church is a weekly opportunity to search your heart alongside others who can correct you and encourage you in your faith—and to find healing and forgiveness together.

Serving for All the Right Reasons

The parts of a body don't exist just for their own sakes. They're designed for a purpose. Just as each part plays a role in the body's survival and health, so each individual participates in the meaning of the church, building others up and making them feel more alive.

As the body of Christ, we must apply all the gifts God gave us to every area of life. Everyone's gifts—even those that are not usually deemed spiritual—have enormous value. Ralph Mattson and Arthur Miller put it this way: "If I am a lawyer, a merchant, a dentist, a farmer, or a machinist with gifts appropriate to those vocations, the Body makes my life of work irrelevant to my life of faith unless it includes all of me when we are together."[12]

This does not mean we should demand a place based on what we think our gifts might be. "You do not announce your gift to the fellowship and create a place for yourself," said Mattson and Miller. "As opportunities arise, you demonstrate your gift and allow the fellowship to confirm your gift and to supply increased opportunities for its use."[13]

Let me state it even more strongly: church is not a place to practice listening to sermons. It is where we practice the life of the kingdom, which is ours now and forever. This is why it is so important not to just look for a church you find entertaining but to find a place where you can participate fully as a member of the body of Christ.

Restoring Our Hope

Being part of a body of believers restores our hope, which is essential to life. Research has shown that having a personal sense of purpose—a sense of what life is all about and one's place within it—radically alters how people cope with their circumstances. Those without purpose report anxiety, disappointment, discouragement, and despair. Those with purpose report joy despite sacrifices they must make, and a sense of energy, satisfaction, and persistence when they run into obstacles.[14]

Multiple studies have shown that participating in a religious community is related to happiness, a sense of well-being, and even physical health. One study discussed in a recent *Psychology Today* article followed over eight thousand people ages forty and older for more than eight years. People who attended church services once a week were 18 percent less likely to die during the study period. Those who attended more than once a week had a 30 percent reduction in the risk of dying.[15] See, all this time you thought those people in church were killing you. Really, they're keeping you alive!

Making Church More Meaningful

Worship. Spiritual growth. Restoration. Service. Hope. Churches that help people grow in these five areas become a significant part of God's kingdom work. Thriving churches help people grow by putting their focus on three areas.

Ensuring That Church Is a Safe Place to Struggle

In Summit Ministries' twelve-day conferences, students often experience personal spiritual breakthroughs. Many confess to significant sins. Our staff rejoices with them but is well aware of how limited our influence is in a short-term program. So we ask, "Who do you know at home that can walk with you through this?" Some say parents or a pastor or an older friend, but most do not have a ready answer.

Here's the uncomfortable truth: for many people, church is not a place they can imagine growing into what they ought to be. They don't feel as if it's a safe place to deal with their struggles; they feel judged for having them.

In their book *unChristian*, David Kinnaman and Gabe Lyons included the results of a survey asking young adults ages sixteen to twenty-nine who do not regularly attend church what characteristics they would use to describe church: 87 percent described the church as "judgmental" and 70 percent described it as "insensitive to others." In fact, 84 percent of these non-church-attenders said they knew a Christian personally, but only 15 percent said they saw any lifestyle differences in those Christians.[16]

If anything justifies the "me and Jesus" mentality, it's hypocrisy. Church doesn't help people *be* good, critics say; it just shows them how to *look* good. It's an assembly line for posers. But measuring the value of God's plan based on how fallen people live is like blaming a car designer for people's poor driving skills.

It's true that people are flawed. Church ought to be the one place where our focus on Jesus puts all our sins in the same light—as forgiven!

God wants me to focus on his Son, not the flaws of people around me. Rather than focusing on what he is doing with others, he wants me to focus on what he is doing in me and desires to do through me. When the apostle Peter asked Jesus about God's plan for another person, Jesus said to him, "What is that to you? You follow me!" (John 21:22). Each person must answer the question "What do you do with Jesus?" I can't answer that question for you, nor can you answer it for me.

Recognizing That Church Is about Everything

Church isn't just one more thing we do. The church is at the center of everything God is doing. It's on a mission—and not an easy one. A friend once described the strategy of a military recruiter speaking to a high school group: "I seriously doubt any of you have what it takes to be a member of our branch of the service, but if you think you do, come talk to me." Guess which military branch had the largest group of students gathering around its information table? We know in our hearts that a worthwhile mission is going to be hard. It can't be accomplished alone. If your life is easy or boring, ask yourself whether you are really on mission. A former air force pilot told me, "If you're not taking flak, you're not over the target."

To make church more robust, we must be honest about how our actions on Sunday morning apply to everything we do the rest of the week. We should assume that the main question people are asking in church is "What does this have to do with where I live and work?" They want to believe in something that makes sense of their lives.

One way churches can help with this is to ask "So what?" about every part of the service. How does this song or this point in the sermon or this Bible teaching make a difference when I'm sitting at my desk or chatting with coworkers around the water cooler?

Making Church a Place to Connect across Generations

According to a Barna Group study, people in their twenties who continue to be involved in church were more than twice as likely to have had a mentor from church while they were in high school.[17] You need an older mentor if you want to grow.[18]

"You need old people," I tell Summit Ministries students. "And they need you." A church should be more like a family reunion and less like a freshman seminar. If you went to a family reunion and everyone there was the same age, that would be, well, bizarre. A family reunion is vibrant because there are older people and babies all bound together by something bigger than any one of them.

The evidence is clear. When older and younger generations interact with one another positively, it reinvigorates the older generation and provides the younger generation with motivation, engagement, prosocial behavior, healthier lifestyles, and greater spiritual development.[19]

It's not "me and Jesus." It's just Jesus.

The "me-ness" of "me and Jesus" is precisely what I need to be rescued from. The only way to find redemption is to admit that I can't save myself. The path to a purpose bigger than myself is outside myself. This is how life works. The biggest dreams are given to characters whose stories are far larger than they ever can tell by themselves.

When I was a college professor, one of my students shared a "my bad" story of a church experience he had. Accompanied by a friend, he visited a new church. As they left, she asked him what he thought of the service. He replied, "I really didn't like the worship time." His friend replied with a hint of mockery, "Well, it's a good thing we weren't worshipping *you*."

When my friend related this incident to me, he laughed and admitted, "She was exactly right. For the entire service I had been focused on what I liked and didn't like. I should have been focused on what God wanted to do in my life—and through me in the lives of others."

Precisely.

The church's greatest impact happens outside its walls, at work and with friends and those in our communities. But how should this happen? Unfortunately, the way believers often communicate spiritual truth to nonbelievers suffers from yet another unquestioned answer, one that sounds pious but risks turning people away from the truth.

Discussion Questions

1. What do you find valuable about belonging to a church?

2. What is it about church community that is challenging?

3. What changes do you need to make in your habits surrounding church—such as attendance, involvement, and attitude?

4. How has the body of Christ helped you through personal struggles?

"Love the Sinner; Hate the Sin"

Rediscovering Truth about Sin and Forgiveness

It was one of those "gotcha" questions interviewers love to spring on unsuspecting Christians. And it worked, catching the talented singer Lauren Daigle off guard. Rising in popularity with both secular and Christian audiences, Daigle had recently won the hearts of American television viewers with a beautifully performed gospel song on the daytime talk show *Ellen*.

Since Daigle's national television debut took place on a show hosted by the openly gay Ellen DeGeneres, it was not surprising that a reporter spied a potential controversy and asked, "Do you feel that homosexuality is a sin?" Daigle replied, "I can't honestly answer on that. In a sense, I have too many people that I love that they are homosexual.... I can't say one way or the other. I'm not God."[1]

The singer found herself in a no-win situation. Daigle's conservative Christian fans were disappointed, and her LGBTQ fans found her ambiguity patronizing. Daigle's words made it seem that God hadn't spoken clearly on the subject or that he hadn't meant what he said.

Amid the ensuing social media firestorm, I felt sorry for Daigle. I've been in her shoes, faced with no-win media questions. *Her publicist should have prepared her for this kind of question,* I thought. When I received training in how to handle antagonistic reporters, the question "Is homosexuality a sin?" was the first one my trainers dinged me with.

On one of my social media accounts, I asked people to put themselves in Daigle's place, with the following rules: give a thirty-second answer—without reflection and without editing—that will be broadcast to the world and remembered forever. One friend replied, "Just thinking how I'd respond and follow the rules stresses me out." Another was less sympathetic: "If you have not thought through sexual ethics by twenty-seven years old, age is not a good excuse.... Her answer does not sound like an artful dodge to me— she simply lacks conviction."

Several people gave it their best shot, though. Many responses were similar to the one given by gospel singer Kim Burrell after her own appearance on *Ellen* was canceled because she referred to the "perverted homosexual spirit" during a sermon. In a Facebook Live session explaining her word choice, Burrell said, "I love you and God loves you. But God hates the sin."[2]

Love the sinner; hate the sin. It's a response I've given many times but am now rethinking after talking with Summit Ministries' instructor Christopher Yuan. As a young man, Christopher was convinced he was gay. He immersed himself in a drug-fueled gay party lifestyle that eventually led to an HIV/AIDS diagnosis and a prison stint for drug dealing. While incarcerated, Christopher found a Bible in a trash can. He started reading it and began a journey to finally understanding what his mother had been praying about for years. Now Christopher teaches at a Bible college. He and his mother travel the United States, talking about biblical sexuality and telling their story of being drawn to Christ.

To be fair, many people say "I love you, but I hate your sin" as a way to express Christ's grace without demeaning the seriousness of sin. Separating the sin from the person makes it seem as if our judgments are somehow less judgmental. But, as Christopher pointed out, when you tell people you love them but hate their sin, "they don't really feel loved! All they hear is what comes after 'but.'"[3]

Christopher also said, "When I lived as a gay man, this was not my 'struggle,' my 'lifestyle,' or my 'choice.' It was simply *who I was*."[4] Our gay friends don't see same-sex relationships as sinful. Rather, they see them as part of their identity, just like the color of their skin or eyes or hair. Imagine saying to someone, "I love you, but I hate your height." Or "the size of your feet." Or "the shape of your face."

You'd have to be pretty stubborn to not acknowledge how this could be hurtful and alienating.

Apply this "love the sinner; hate the sin" phrasing to common sins such as lying and pride, and it's easier to see how it can feel like a spiritual hit-and-run: "I love you, but I hate that you are a liar" or "I love you, but I hate that you are a self-centered jerk." That's not the way we would confront people if we really did love them.

Yet we face a quandary: the Bible is clear about sin. What we do and who we do it with are tied to how we bear God's image.

Somehow we must find our way between two extremes, with one side seeing the Bible as a collection of legal codes Christians must enforce, as if we are handing out parking tickets, and the other expressing a timid unwillingness to proclaim the life-changing power of the gospel.

"Love the sinner; hate the sin" is an unquestioned answer we should probably abandon—and not just because it is insensitive. Rather, it's because God's approach to sin in the Bible is vastly richer and more hopeful than such a statement could ever convey.

The essential story is this: God is against anything that keeps us from more fully bearing his image. Sin isn't just doing things we shouldn't do or failing to do things we should. It goes deeper. When we grasp the bigger picture of what God is doing in the world, we gain the power to abandon simplistic pronouncements and instead embrace a way of talking about God's plan that turns people to Christ rather than away from him.

Where Does This Unquestioned Answer Come From?

In a *USA Today* editorial about gospel singer Kim Burrell's pronouncements about homosexuality, Jonathan Merritt traced the phrase "Love the sinner; hate the sin" back to the church father Augustine of Hippo.[5] As a young man Augustine had lived a life of sinful pleasure but converted to Christianity after hearing a childlike voice say, "Pick it up and read it." He found a Bible and stumbled onto this passage: "Put on the Lord Jesus Christ, and make no provision for the flesh, to gratify its desires" (Rom. 13:14). Five years later, Augustine became a priest, then the bishop of Hippo, a city in Africa.

Much of Augustine's work survives, including a statement he made while trying to settle a quarrel among the Hippo monastery's nuns: "Just as severity is ready to punish the sins that it finds, so love does not want to find any to punish."[6] Every parent understands this. You need to be prepared to discipline wrongdoing, but you hope your kids behave responsibly, because you'd rather have peace and harmony from the start.

Yet the root of "Love the sinner; hate the sin" is found in the rich soil of Scripture itself. In Matthew 5:43–44 Jesus said, "You have heard that it was said, 'You shall love your neighbor and hate your enemy.' But I say to you, Love your enemies and pray for those who persecute you." The apostle Paul tied together love for others and an avoidance of sin: "Let love be genuine. Abhor what is evil; hold fast to what is good" (Rom. 12:9).

God loves us. God hates sin. That's hardly controversial. But if we're honest, we'll realize that we're more likely to say "Love the sinner; hate the sin" in response to sins we don't think we will commit. There's a hint of self-righteousness in it, as if we're saying, "God may be mildly irritated by *my* sins, but he is *really* upset by *yours*."

Any sense that we can make ourselves right before God, though, should be erased by realizing that on our own we are just as doomed as anyone whose sins we condemn. The gospel's message is that we *all* would be destined for an eternity without God apart from the powerful work of Christ.

The Bible isn't just a list of rules. It's a revelation from God about what he wants, how we all fall short, and how we can be redeemed. God has rescued us! It's as if, while toppling headlong over a cliff, we find ourselves grasped by a strong, firm hand and pulled back to safety. If we don't marvel at what we've been rescued from, then we probably don't appreciate the effects of the law of gravity—or in this case, "the law of sin and death" (Rom. 8:2). I say this not because it's a theological belief that makes sense to me but because the Bible spells out clearly who we are, what is wrong with us, and how we can be saved.

Who Are We?

In order to fully appreciate our rescue, we need to know what it was like to not be lost. Creation begins with God's first recorded words: "Let there be light" (Gen. 1:3). It's a simple sentence. No hammering, no sawing. Just the sound of God's voice turning *nothing* into *something*. Then, after creating the seas, fish, birds, and land animals, God said, "Let us make man in our image, after our likeness. And let them have dominion over the fish of the sea and over the birds of the heavens and over the livestock and over all the earth and over every creeping thing that creeps on the earth" (v. 26).

Image bearing was a familiar concept in the ancient Near Eastern culture in which the book of Genesis was written. An image symbolized authority over a certain domain. Images of a conquering king reminded people who was in charge.

Victorious kings would *never* say, "Now you are just like me. Please share in my greatness." Such a thing was not done. But God is like no other king, and he did it anyway. He took the dust of earth, breathed into it, and created a living, moving bearer of his own image. Not only that, but whenever people did make statues of him (or other gods), God condemned such efforts as idolatry.

Bearing God's image is more than church-speak. It's a statement about what *is*. Not just for those who believe but for all who have ever lived or ever will. We are not just "matter in motion," as many atheists believe. We're something far more.

Our souls are that "something far more." In Genesis 2:7, God breathed and man became a living soul. Our bodies are physical, but our souls tell us that our physical beings are not all we are. Our bodies are alive, but our souls *know* we are alive. Our bodies experience nerve impulses, but our souls know we aren't merely machines reacting to our surroundings. We reason, prepare, reflect, create, choose, talk, and love. We have a life force that is more than mere animation. It is soulish.

As image bearers of God, we take on God's "shape." As sons and daughters resemble their parents, we resemble God.[7] God's image isn't just a state of being. It's also a state of doing. After creating humans, God put them in the garden to work and keep it. The Hebrew words for "work" and "keep" mean "to work or serve" and "to exercise great care over."[8] In creation God was saying, "I love life! Blossoming and birthing and hatching and teeming and swarming bring me joy. Now that you're like me, I want you to want what I want."

Our first parents lived in this paradise with God, doing what breathed life into them and bringing God joy. But then something went very, very wrong.

What Is Wrong with Us?

Almost everyone would agree that there is something wrong with us. Things are not as they ought to be. A glance at trends and statistics reveals the truth about our world's condition:

- People are more likely to die from drug overdoses than from car crashes or shootings.[9]
- Mental illness and emotional distress are at an all-time high.[10]
- Major depression is rising among all age-groups, as is the suicide rate.[11]
- Communities are breaking down as violent crime and murder rates remain troublingly high.
- While total wealth is growing, about 15 percent of Americans still live in poverty, a level that has remained largely unchanged despite trillions of dollars of welfare spending.[12]
- Children have become the most vulnerable among us, with levels of physical abuse, sexual abuse, malnourishment, and neglect at historic highs.
- Almost a third of sex-trafficking victims are children.[13]

Anyone who says that things are fine isn't facing reality.

The Bible's account of human brokenness begins in Genesis 3 with the heartbreaking account of how our first parents, Adam and Eve, tried to slough off their image-bearing capacity but found underneath only naked embarrassment, not the profound wisdom they had hoped for.

In the biblical account of the fall, God pronounced a curse on the man and woman along with the serpent who coaxed them into such a shameful state (vv. 14–19). At first this seems like an over-reaction. God lost his temper and decided to forever ruin the lives of his precious children. But it's more a statement about what happens when we tell God, "Leave us alone." Without God's touch, what once had been pleasurable became painful. What had been fruitful became barren. The fall massively affected the world and everything in it.

Throughout the Bible, in both the Old and the New Testaments, the word *sin* means "to depart from God's way." Jeremiah 6:16 says, "Thus says the LORD: 'Stand by the roads, and look, and ask for the ancient paths, where the good way is; and walk in it, and find rest for your souls. But they said, "We will not walk in it."'"

As we wander further from God, sin overtakes our souls in the same way parasites take over a body.[14] A parasite is an organism that survives by living inside a body and stealing the nutrition the body needs to stay alive. Lying, for example, couldn't exist unless we humans had the capacity to tell the truth. When we mislead others into believing what is not actually true, a parasite enters our souls, where it drains us of life and makes us—and others—miserable.

How Can We Be Fixed?

What do we do about sin? When a creature is afflicted with parasites, the prescription is to remove them, not to kill the host. If the host is unhealthy, restoring it to health must be part of the plan. To do this with the parasite of sin, though, we must know something of the state to which we hope to be restored.[15]

Pretending to be okay does not redeem us. Money, power, sex appeal, and adventure cannot save us. Look around. We have become like the things we worship: unstable, shallow, and uncaring.

Fortunately, rescue is at hand. It begins through an encounter with God's glory. In the light of God's glory, the Old Testament prophet Isaiah instantly saw his own fallenness. "Woe is me!" he cried out. "For I am lost; for I am a man of unclean lips, and I dwell in the midst of a people of unclean lips; for my eyes have seen the King, the LORD of hosts!" (Isa. 6:5).

God's glory instantly scours away any illusion that we are okay or that we can make ourselves godlike or that we can bargain our way out of our predicament. The white-hot hum of God's glory burns against anything standing in the way of our fully bearing the image of the always good, always merciful, and always faithful God.

The path to repentance is through encountering God's glory. The New Testament word for "repentance" is the Greek word *metanoia*, which refers to rejecting an inferior way of life and seeking enlightenment.

Transparency is not enough. Being honest about our shortcomings is not the same thing as renouncing them and setting off in the opposite direction. Repentance is a joyful—not a fearful—embrace of God's glory. As Pastor Timothy Keller said, "Fear-based repentance makes us hate ourselves. Joy-based repentance makes us hate the sin."[16] According to Scripture, God's kindness leads us to repentance of the right sort (Rom. 2:4).

In repenting, we gain the right to be called children of God (John 1:12). We are set free from spiritual condemnation (Rom. 8:1). We become heirs with Christ (Rom. 8:16–17) and one spirit with him (1 Cor. 6:17). We are a new creation (2 Cor. 5:17) and are blessed with every spiritual blessing (Eph. 1:3).

This, in turn, changes how we see everything, especially other people.

What Must We Do Now?

"I forgive you," Mike said simply, "and thank you." I felt relieved at his words yet a little self-conscious, as I feel when I hand the keys of my muddy, dog-hair-covered Jeep to a sharply dressed valet. Mike and I went to college together. In our student government he was honorable and treated others with respect. Yet during some petty conflict, I had bad-mouthed him and damaged his reputation. My actions had bothered me for two years.

Having recently become a Christian, I felt deeply convicted by my past sin and obsessed with righting past wrongs. Romans 12:18 says, "If possible, so far as it depends on you, live peaceably with all." To me that meant making a list of those I had offended and trying to make amends.

The more I reflected on my past sin, the more I grieved. I recalled things I hadn't considered for years, such as the time in first grade when my friend pushed a girl into a puddle—I still remember her name—and despite her tears I stood by and did nothing to help. I recalled the time in eighth grade when I got caught cheating in band class. Instead of apologizing and vowing to change my dishonest ways, I angrily decided to be more careful about getting caught in the future.

Dozens more examples came to mind. I felt overwhelmed. Fog had cleared, and I found myself treading water in an ocean of wrongs.

I started through my list. Some people I couldn't track down. Others graciously offered forgiveness. Still others seemed baffled or upset by my call. I understand. If someone unexpectedly reached out seeking forgiveness, I might feel put on the spot. Hearing from that person might open old wounds or make me feel suspicious.

Thankfully God never reacts this way. As 1 John 1:9 says, "If we confess our sins, he is faithful and just to forgive us our sins and to cleanse us from all unrighteousness." Knowing keenly the value of God's forgiveness in his own life, David wrote, "As far as the east is from the west, so far does he remove our transgressions from us" (Ps. 103:12).

As I sought forgiveness from others, I grew to understand how I affect them. I had thought a lot about bearing God's image personally, and I began seeing what it meant to project God's image to others. This understanding gave me new insight into a conversation Jesus had with a lawyer who asked, "Teacher, what shall I do to inherit eternal life?" (Luke 10:25). Jesus answered with a question: "What is written in the Law? How do you read it?" (v. 26). The lawyer replied that we should love God with heart, soul, strength, and mind and should love our neighbors as ourselves. Jesus affirmed this (vv. 27–28).

But as cross-examining lawyers often do, this one had "just one more question." He asked, "Who is my neighbor?" (v. 29). Jesus answered by telling a story about a man, robbed and beaten, who was ignored by righteous men but tended to by a despised Samaritan (vv. 30–35).

Every Jewish person knew the revered teaching of Moses about loving God with our entire beings (Deut. 6:5). For many it had become an unquestioned answer, a mantra to recite, not necessarily a way of life.

Believers then and now need to remember that love for God involves loving what God loves. If we love God richly, our love for him spills out into love for our neighbors. Even the ones we hate. Even the ones who hate us.

If I'm honest, embracing the slogan "Love the sinner; hate the sin" was my way of trying to appear loving while subtly putting my thumb on the scale and judging others as less righteous than myself. The truth is, apart from God's mercy I'm a lot more like the worst person who has ever lived than I am the man God designed me to be. Instead of making pronouncements such as "Love the sinner; hate the sin," our Summit speaker Christopher Yuan suggested engaging others directly about their identity by asking questions such as "Who are you? Tell me more about you."[17]

Asking questions is an especially powerful way to engage when you're challenged. For example, if someone were to ask you, "Is being gay a sin?" you could ask, "How do you define sin?" and "What does it mean to be gay?" When someone asks, "Do you think gays are going to hell?" you could reply, "What's your understanding of who deserves God's judgment?"[18]

Asking questions is how Jesus approached many tough conversations. Remember, Jesus asked the lawyer, "What is written in the

Law? How do you read it?" (Luke 10:26). It's not that Jesus didn't know the answer but that he wanted the lawyer to think through the issue with him. Jesus chose to relate, not merely react.

This is not to say we should hem and haw about truth. We must take a stand. In tough moments I've taken the late Chuck Colson's comment to heart: "Orthodoxy often requires us to be hard precisely where the world is soft, and soft where the world is hard.... In every way that matters, Christianity is an affront to the world; it is countercultural."[19]

———

When we have God's viewpoint on creation, the fall, and redemption, we approach others with a recognition of our own ghastly fallenness and Jesus's unimaginable offer of grace. Pride flees, replaced with a recollection of falling headlong into the abyss, only to find ourselves safely in the grip of the One we had betrayed.

I also can't assume that my restoration is complete or that I can take credit for my progress. The supreme irony of sin is that attempting to free myself only leaves me more ensnared. Every day God is shaping me into the image of his Son. God himself is involved, stepping in against anything that separates me from him.

Having an identity in Christ resonates strongly in a day when people root their identity in things they can control or in a perceived ability to have it all together. At Summit Ministries I tell students, "Your sin is *how* you are, not *who* you are. Your identity is in Christ as an image bearer of God. Look at what God has done for us! We do not have to be imprisoned by our sin. Through Jesus we can live lives that are fully pleasing to God."

Christ's offer of redemption extends to everyone, even to a wretch like me. That's the gospel's good news for each of us. I believe it, but it also leaves me with a question I've wrestled with for a long time: Is the gospel relevant only to each person's salvation, or does it speak to the life of the world? Some say Jesus's offer of a personal relationship ends the need for religion. Others say the gospel is part of a larger religious worldview that should be applied to every area of life. Relationship? Religion? These are questions I pondered standing in front of a tiny cell in the worst place on earth, where a tragic event set in motion an unstoppable force for good.

Discussion Questions

1. Are there people you need to forgive? Are there people from whom you need to ask forgiveness?

2. How can you have a gospel witness to people who have been hurt by this cliché?

3. How should the Bible's message about our identity change the way we think about sin, forgiveness, and sanctification (especially in relation to restoration, evangelism, etc.)?

4. In what do you find your identity?

"Christianity Is a Relationship, Not a Religion"

Rediscovering Truth about Worldview

"ARBEIT MACHT FREI," read the sign, bars of iron twisted into words. The translation: "Work sets you free."

I felt a cold knot in my stomach. It was so mocking, so evil, this sign. The people once imprisoned here were slaves. Almost none were set free, except by death.

I stood at the entrance to Auschwitz, the notorious Nazi death camp. Next to me, my eleven-year-old son surveyed the scene, wide eyed. *Was it a mistake to bring him here at his age?* I wondered.

The autumn sun gently illuminated the manicured lawns and well-kept buildings that lay just beyond where we stood. Decades before, on a day like this, thousands of Polish people and Jews from all over Europe would have been systematically tortured and killed by poison gas, hanging, firing squads, suffocation, sickening medical experiments, and starvation.

Stricken, we shuffled from one exhibit to the next, observing torture chambers and room after room of evidence. One exhibit displayed bales of "cloth" made from human hair. Another featured an enormous pile of shoes. I saw a woman's colorful shoe right on top, the sort one might wear to a picnic. Some shoes were tiny. I imagined parents loosening them with trembling hands as SS guards screamed, "Hurry up! Get in the showers. You must be disinfected!"

What kind of people would commit such evil? I asked myself.

The answer is an uncomfortable one. Nazism was not a spontaneous outburst from a horde of angry peasants. It was a movement made up of people who were startlingly ordinary. Appraising the mental state of Holocaust architect Adolf Eichmann, the court psychiatrist pronounced him a "completely normal man, more normal, at any rate, than I am after examining him."[1]

Nazism was more than the political and economic system of national socialism. It functioned as a religion based in Germanic mythology, with a system of good and evil (Aryans versus Jews and other "undesirables"), a savior (Adolf Hitler), and a desired future (the thousand-year Reich). Nazism turned ordinary people into mass murderers by convincing them that they were part of a legendary cause that was destined to change the world.

What hope is there, especially in a world where such people possess brutal force without moral constraint?

As our tour group filed into block 11 and made our way down a shadowy corridor, I found my answer in a tiny, dimly lit cell. This is where, I would come to learn, something wretched happened that began to turn the tide from evil to good.

In July 1941 the Auschwitz deputy commandant selected ten men to be starved to death in retribution for a prisoner escaping. He began calling out the numbers of those randomly chosen to be condemned.

"Prisoner 5659," he announced loudly.

With a shock of recognition, prisoner 5659, Franciszek Gajowniczek (Fran-SEE-sheck Guy-OWD-nee-sheck) cried out in lament for his family. Hearing Gajowniczek, a stooped, balding prisoner stepped forward, boldly addressing the commandant: "I am a Catholic priest from Poland. I would like to take his place, because he has a wife and children."[2]

Unbelievably the commandant permitted the switch. "I could only thank him with my eyes," Gajowniczek later recalled, describing the moment he gazed at the man who had offered to sacrifice his life. "I, the condemned, am to live and someone else willingly and voluntarily offers his life for me—a stranger. Is this some dream?"[3]

It wasn't a dream. The priest's name was Maximilian Kolbe. He had become Auschwitz prisoner 16670 for sheltering thousands of Jews and other Poles in his monastery and for being a journalist, publisher, and intellectual.

The SS guards roughly shoved the ten men into an impossibly small cell, where they would be denied food and water until dead. Kolbe led them in praying and singing hymns.

One by one the men died. After two weeks only Kolbe and three others remained alive. Irritated and wanting the cell for other prisoners, guards injected each man with carbolic acid. When he came to Kolbe, the forty-seven-year-old priest weakly offered his arm. Within minutes he was dead.

After the war, word of Kolbe's sacrifice spread to the nearby city of Krakow, where a young seminary student named Karol Wojtyła (voy-TEE-wah) listened in awe. Wojtyła vowed to honor Kolbe's courage and redeem his death.[4]

You may have never heard the name Karol Wojtyła, but you are almost certainly familiar with the name he took upon being elected leader of the Roman Catholic Church in 1978: Pope John Paul II.

The year after his election, John Paul II visited Poland for nine days, delivering dozens of speeches to throngs of admirers. At the time, the nation was strictly ruled by a Communist dictator. Yet John Paul II didn't mention economics or politics in his speeches.[5] Instead, in many he spoke of Maximilian Kolbe, the man who through faith had gained the victory over a system cruelly constructed to destroy faith itself. "Do not be afraid," the pontiff encouraged.

The courage of the Poles swelled as they realized, *We are not alone!* A year later, the Solidarity labor movement formed. From that point there was no turning back. Eventually Poland's Communist government fell, as did one Communist regime after another. At last, with a mighty crash, the once great USSR—under which twenty to sixty million people were killed—ceased to exist.[6]

The revolution that began Europe's Communist nightmare was a political and economic one. The revolution that brought it down was a spiritual one.

As an old man, Franciszek Gajowniczek met Pope John Paul II. The photo of their meeting shows the former Polish army sergeant clasping the hand of the vibrant pontiff, not quite able to meet his gaze. They say a picture is worth a thousand words, but no photo can adequately tell this story: a man whose life had been spared by an unexpected sacrifice, leaning into the embrace of a revered spiritual leader who, inspired by that sacrifice, proclaimed to a world in chains, "Do not be afraid."

To the Nazis, Maximilian Kolbe was prisoner 16670. To history, he became the simple priest who laid down his life and helped topple an empire.

At the conclusion of our Auschwitz tour, my son and I boarded the silver Mercedes van for the hour-long journey back to Krakow. Whizzing past fields and forests, some in our group played cards and laughed. My son and I sat in silence. I could only think of Psalm 10:8: "He waits in ambush near the villages; he kills the innocent in secret places. His eyes are on the lookout for the helpless" (HCSB). Would I have stood up for the helpless as Kolbe did? Would I have had the courage to stand against the unyielding tide of history?

Even as a Christian I had seen myself as not particularly religious. It seemed to me that when people develop systems around their beliefs, they often end up pushing others to the margins in their fight for control.

"Forget all the systems and the rules," I would tell people, recalling my own childhood experience in a harsh fundamentalist school.

"It's about Jesus and your personal relationship with him. Think relationship, not religion."

Visiting Auschwitz and seeing what happened when Nazis religiously lived out their beliefs served only to confirm my belief that religion hurts people. But I was conflicted. What about the religious commitment of Maximilian Kolbe or of John Paul II, who as leader of the Roman Catholic Church fought against totalitarianism and injustice?

I realized that my "relationship versus religion" mantra had become an unquestioned answer that kept my faith at a shallow level. Certainly it was right to focus on a personal relationship with Jesus. Yet I suspected that by focusing only on *my* relationship with Jesus, I had developed a self-centered faith. Such a faith could have never gathered the courage or intellectual resources to stand against evil the way Maximilian Kolbe and John Paul II had done.

Even though it is a mantra I've often recited, I'm coming to see the statement "Christianity is a relationship, not a religion" as an unsatisfying unquestioned answer. We need both relationship and religion, assuming we properly understand each. The Bible's teachings about faith are deeply personal, but they also form a worldview that has changed the world forever.

Where Does This Unquestioned Answer Come From?

Recently I googled "What is a good use for a church?" and found several articles on "repurposed" churches. One was a home. Another housed a data center. Churches had been converted into a bookstore, a bar, a skate park, a fraternity house, and even an atheist meeting center.

Short of a revival, developers will soon have more inventory to work with. Young adults today increasingly claim no religious affiliation. Almost 40 percent of Americans ages eighteen to twenty-nine do not link themselves with a religious tradition. In the United States, the United Methodist Church has lost half of the fifteen million members it claimed in 1970.[7] The Southern Baptist church claims fifteen million members, but less than half of those attend services.[8]

But this doesn't mean people are without faith. The majority of Americans say they believe in God, and the percentage who tell pollsters they are "spiritual but not religious" has grown to 27 percent of the population.[9] A seismic shift has occurred as people forsake doctrinal distinctions and orders of worship in search of a way to personally connect with God.

To many Christians, shifting to focus on "relationship, not religion" is a significant improvement over the old system of rules and duties. There is no one like Jesus, who proclaimed freedom from burdensome regulations, they say. Forget those 613 arcane Old Testament laws. The Messiah has come! Jesus saves.

This contrast between relationship and religion is vividly communicated by spoken-word artist Jefferson Bethke, whose YouTube video on the topic has received more than thirty-four million views. Bethke packed a lot into his four-minute piece, including riffs on the sad ways Christians have polluted Jesus's message. At the climax of his performance, he declared,

Because religion says "Do"; Jesus says "Done."
Religion says "Slave"; Jesus says "Son."[10]

These powerful lines rightly spotlight the personal nature of salvation in Jesus. In our darkest moments, we don't need more rules. We need a redeemer.

Yet to pit relationship against religion is to highlight Jesus's unique message at the expense of the Bible's powerful claims about the reality that situates it. Doing so makes "me" more important than "we."

If what the Bible says is valid, then we know one thing for certain: a life of faith is *not* about me. It's about everyone and everything everywhere. God isn't just my friend; he's the one who answers humanity's most profound questions about the cause, nature, and purpose of the universe.

Rather than place relationship and religion at odds with each other, I'd like to offer a different perspective: Jesus didn't change God's plan; he fulfilled it. From the beginning God has shown himself to be a personal, relational God. He reveals the truth about the cause, nature, and purpose of the universe in a way that brings hope and healing to the whole world. In this sense, Christianity is a religion that intentionally speaks to the life of the world. Not only is it a form of worship and a set of moral guidelines; it is also a worldview—a view *of* the world and *for* the world.

Christianity Is a Worldview

Religion and *worldview* are similar terms. Usually people use the word *religion* to refer to religious practices such as a form of worship or moral guidelines. *Worldview* usually describes how that religion's ideas about where everything came from (cause), what is real (nature), and how we ought to live (purpose) come together to form a vision for society. The backdrop of the Bible is a historical narrative that explains how we got here, why things aren't working out the way they ought to, and how Jesus makes it all new.

For years I've emphasized to our students at Summit Ministries that ideas have consequences. Ideas form our beliefs, shape our convictions, and solidify into habits. We each live as if certain ideas are true, even if we've not given them a lot of thought. From this viewpoint the central question is not whether religion is a good thing but whether a religion's claims are true. As C. S. Lewis said, "Religion involves a series of statements about facts, which must be either true or false. If they are true, one set of conclusions will follow about the right sailing of the human fleet: if they are false, quite a different set."[11]

The Bible's claims about reality are justified true beliefs. The problem is not that the truth is unclear; it's that our perception is distorted. Even for those who trust Jesus as their Savior, it takes training and discipline to discern the truth.

Imagine walking around a crowded room and then being asked to write down every detail you remember. Everyone would remember a few things, but a trained detective would remember much more. Why? Because of intense practice in distinguishing between clues and background noise. Based on their assumptions about reality, detectives have developed a mental checklist for seeing clearly what others miss.[12]

From beginning to end, the Bible proclaims three realities that enable us to see God, ourselves, and everything else more clearly.

Reality 1: Creation

From the first verses of the Bible, we can see that there is one God, not many. The universe had a beginning and has not always existed. God himself superintended every aspect of creation. Nothing about it is an accident. God created by *fiat*, a Latin word meaning "let it be done."[13] What God wants *happens*. What God says *goes*. Even *nothing* became *something* when God told it to.

In creation God didn't just reveal his plan; he revealed *himself*. God is a person, not a thing. God isn't pure energy, as various other worldviews maintain. Pure energy does not create—it explodes. God is the one who harnessed energy to purposeful ends. His presence sustains the world (Col. 1:16–17). The universe speaks of God's creativity and existence; it speaks the language of God.[14]

As we've already seen, a significant part of the creation account is God forming humans in his image. This is far different from Egyptian creation stories in which humans are slaves of the gods and only special classes of people (such as pharaohs) bear God's image. Imagine the Israelites' amazement at learning, after more than four hundred years of captivity in Egypt, that their identity was based on bearing God's image rather than that of their masters.[15]

Reality 2: The Fall

Things function best according to their design. If we ignore God's design for eating, for example, our bodies function poorly. In a larger sense, ignoring creation's balance leads to overharvesting and choking the life out of the earth. Ignoring design breaks faith with the

Designer. The Bible calls it "sin," which is a betrayal of the one whose image we bear.

Sin is not just *out there*; it is *in here*. It affects structures as well as persons; whole communities—indeed whole nations—fall in its wake. Sin never heals; it only corrupts. Sin attacks our humanity, spiraling us endlessly downward. We can see where sin's path leads, but like addicts, we attack anything and anyone standing in the way of the next fix. Self-destruction is our bent. Some suffer through disastrous lifestyle choices; others suffocate on haughtiness and contempt.

Reality 3: Redemption

Some see God as a harsh judge who, after a couple of millennia of contemplation, decided to punish his own Son for the sin of humanity. This picture falls far short of the full truth. In Scripture, God revealed himself as the Redeemer buying back his wayward creation. We see his redemptive nature in the garden when he told the serpent, "I will put enmity between you and the woman, and between your offspring and her offspring; he shall bruise your head, and you shall bruise his heel" (Gen. 3:15). God took a basic human act—standing—and transformed it into a metaphorical weapon for destroying slithering evil. The one who deceived at the beginning will be crushed at the end (Rom. 16:20; Rev. 12:9).

Redemption opens our eyes to see from God's unlimited perspective rather than our own limited one. According to the apostle Paul, to understand what God wants from us, we must identify the world's patterns, refuse to conform to them, and have our patterns of living transformed to be pleasing to God (Rom. 12:2).

Creation. Fall. Redemption. This narrative—how we got here, what went wrong, and how Jesus redeems it—forms a set of beliefs about the cause, nature, and purpose of the universe. These are profoundly religious truths that come alive through relationship and can't help but shape the world around us.

What Must We Do Now?

"Somewhere along the way, the Jesus movement got hijacked," said the controversial pastor Rob Bell. "I actually think Jesus would be absolutely mortified that somebody started a religion in his name."[16] Bell's statement is a common way to describe the "relationship, not religion" framing.

But if the work of Christ forms a set of beliefs about the cause, nature, and purpose of the universe, then "relationship or religion" obscures the full picture of what Christ has done. Take marriage as an example (as the Bible often does). If you're married, the two of you are made one by a covenantal bond that transforms your relationship into a new reality affecting everything in your life and moving outward to the world. If you describe your spouse as "a person I hang out with," it would be a factual statement but one that obscures the larger truth of what your marriage represents.

Some people fear that focusing on religion or worldview makes a Jesus-focused faith too intellectual and restrictive. It takes the mystery out of it. If we properly understand who Jesus is, though, we realize that a Jesus-focused faith offers a positive vision that not only *describes* reality for everyone everywhere but also *prescribes* how life works best.

Put another way, the Bible's message does not end with relationship. It *begins* with that. Relationship isn't something God does—it is what he *is* by his very nature. A Jesus-focused faith opens up reality rather than narrowing it. Here's how:

A Jesus-focused faith transforms what we know. Jesus is the one who opens the door of reality. He is "the fulness of the Godhead" (Col. 2:9 KJV). He is the Word through whom knowledge about God and the world is revealed (John 1:1). Putting Christian theology and philosophy into practice through a relationship with Jesus results in salvation of the soul (Matt. 16:26), enlightenment of the mind, and purpose in life.

A Jesus-focused faith transforms how we live personally. Jesus Christ is "the true light" (John 1:9). In his light we can see the difference between right and wrong and gain power to pursue what is right. He is also "the life" (1:4; 11:25). All of life takes on meaning because of him, and we can have purpose in an aimless world.

A Jesus-focused faith transforms how we live with others. Of all the ways God could have revealed himself to the world, he chose the one way all human beings could understand: he sent his Son (Isa. 9:6; Luke 1:31–32). Family and relationship are at the heart of God's plan. Putting Christian living into practice encourages strong families and guards against widespread drug use, crime, unemployment, poverty, and disease.

A Jesus-focused faith transforms governance. God hates the perversion of justice. Throughout Scripture the Messiah is characterized as a lawgiver (Gen. 49:10; Isa. 9:7). Government isn't God. It doesn't *grant* us rights—it merely secures what we have been given by the one the Bible calls the King of kings and Lord of lords (Isa. 9:6; Luke 1:33; Rev. 17:14). Jesus doesn't demand that we take over government and rule in his name. Rather, in his name we insist that people be treated with dignity and freed to fulfill their God-given potential. Jesus is the true basis of human rights.

A Jesus-focused faith transforms productivity. Throughout Scripture the Lord is described as the owner of all things (Ps. 24:1; 1 Cor. 10:26). We serve as stewards to cultivate the things and people in our realms of influence. From beginning to end, it's all about Jesus (Rev. 1:8). Putting biblical principles of economics into practice results in prosperity for the greatest number of people, while humanity's best strategies result only in generational poverty.

The story of Jesus is the story of everything. It's simple enough that even a child can understand it. As Sally Lloyd-Jones wrote to her young readers in *The Jesus Storybook Bible,*

> The Bible is most of all a Story. It's an adventure story about a young Hero who comes from a far country to win back his lost treasure. It's a love story about a brave Prince who leaves his palace, his throne—everything—to rescue the one he loves. It's like the most wonderful of fairy tales that has come true in real life!...
>
> It takes the whole Bible to tell this Story. And at the center of the Story, there is a baby. Every Story in the Bible whispers his name. He is like the missing piece in a puzzle—the piece that makes all the other pieces fit together, and suddenly you can see a beautiful picture.[17]

Yes, we want all people to be restored in their relationship with God. But we also want to encourage everyone everywhere to live as if God's message is true. That means we need to take religion as seriously as we take relationship.

—

Stirred by his faith, Maximilian Kolbe courageously embraced a death sentence. Moved by Kolbe's sacrifice, Karol Wojtyła inspired millions of people oppressed by Communism to have that kind of courage. Galvanized, the oppressed rose up in a spiritual revolution, winning freedom with almost no bloodshed.

What happens in the spiritual world affects the physical world. God designed it that way. A personal relationship with Jesus comes to life in a religion that gives us true insight into the cause, nature, and purpose of the universe—a worldview that offers hope and healing to the whole world.

Chiune Sugihara demonstrated this. He was a Japanese diplomat to Lithuania during World War II. Upon hearing what was happening at the hands of the Nazis, he began issuing visas allowing Jews to "transit" through Japan on their way to somewhere else, even though there *was* no "somewhere else."

Japan had ordered Sugihara not to issue visas to people without visas to travel on to another country. Sugihara chose to obey his conscience rather than the directive given by his government. He wrote visas by hand at a rate of three hundred per day for more than a month, saving between six thousand and ten thousand Jews from the Holocaust.[18] "Rescue those who are being taken away to death," says

Proverbs 24:11. Sugihara didn't do this just because he could win converts. "Do what's right because it's right, and leave it alone," he said.[19]

If what the Bible says is valid, then it's about everyone and everything everywhere. Neither the word *relationship* nor the word *religion* sufficiently describes the awesome work of God in sending Jesus. He is fully God, the one through whom we know God, the one who is crushing evil and rebuffing its ability to destroy what is most important about us.

A Jesus-focused faith begins with a personal relationship and expands into a set of beliefs about everything that affects everything. This doesn't mean it's always easy to figure out. As we will see in the next chapter, nowhere is this truer than in the arena of social justice, where Christians trying to live out their faith have gotten caught up in an agenda that takes the exact opposite approach of what the Bible intends.

Discussion Questions

1. What was your experience with Jesus growing up?

2. Has Christianity always been familiar to you? If so, was there more of an emphasis on relationship or on religion?

3. How would you define *religion*?

4. Do you agree that religion is an integral part of being a Christian? Why?

7

"Jesus Was a Social Justice Warrior"

Rediscovering Truth about Justice

I can't wait for this race to be over, I grumbled to myself as my phone's shrill alarm sounded well before daylight. While in my final days of preparing to run a marathon, I found myself in El Paso, Texas, for a speaking engagement. The schedule was tight; my only opportunity for a training run was *really* early in the morning. Stepping out into the cool morning air, I pushed my earbuds in tight and let the music wake me as I shuffled up a trail toward a mountain outlined in the predawn light.

Suddenly I was struck by a strong impression, almost a voice: "Turn around—*now.*" Fully alert, I chose another route and completed my run.

Later, when I told an El Paso resident about my experience, his face went pale. "If you had continued up that trail, you almost certainly would have been stripped and robbed by banditos," he said. "There is a border war here. You need to be very careful."

He must be exaggerating, I thought. A quick online search showed that he wasn't. One ominous news article declared, "Juarez, a city of 1.3 million hugging the border with El Paso, Tex., may now be the most dangerous place in the world—riskier even than Baghdad or Kandahar."[1] Rival drug gangs were killing one another along with anyone who got in their way, the article said. Thousands of people died each year.

The tragedy had escalated a few months before my visit. Police found two adults shot to death in a Toyota RAV4 SUV, a crying baby strapped in the back seat. Police identified the victims as a US consulate employee, Lesley A. Enriquez, and her husband. Just twenty-five years old, Lesley was four months pregnant with her second child.[2]

The targeting of a US citizen got the attention of US officials in Washington, DC. They swung into action, charging thirty-eight people they believed to be responsible for the violence plaguing the city. Among those captured was Arturo Gallegos Castrellon, who boasted of ordering the deaths of thousands.

Enter Brian Skaret, a Justice Department attorney. Facing the risk of retaliation by Castrellon's followers, Skaret and his team successfully prosecuted dozens of the thugs terrorizing Juárez, ensuring that they would never again see freedom. With many of the criminals behind bars, the murder rate dropped by 80 percent and the once bullied city of Juárez began to heal.

As an attorney for the US Department of Justice, Brian continues to prosecute violent criminals. He and his son have also started a project to support the children of Colombian police officers slain in the line of duty. Brian's work aims to set things right.

Setting things right. That's a pretty good biblical definition of justice. It's something God cares deeply about. In commands outlined for ancient Israel, the Bible says, "You shall do no injustice in court. You shall not be partial to the poor or defer to the great, but in righteousness shall you judge your neighbor" (Lev. 19:15). Proverbs 24:12 says, "If you say, 'Behold, we did not know this,' does not he who weighs the heart perceive it? Does not he who keeps watch over your soul know it, and will he not repay man according to his work?"

God loves justice (Ps. 33:5). It is a constant theme in Scripture. If you aren't concerned about justice, you should ask yourself whether you have God's heart for the world.

The kind of justice the Bible talks about requires action, not just good intentions. It is hard work and requires constant vigilance, as Brian's work demonstrates. Discussions about justice often become uncomfortable, though, because political and social groups use justice as a weapon to claim moral superiority and shame those with whom they disagree. This "God is on my side, and he's against you" refrain threatens to tear us apart at a moment in history when the Bible's teachings on justice are more needed than ever.

Of all the unquestioned answers in this book, the claim "Jesus was a social justice warrior" may be the most fraught with controversy. To address it, we need to figure out what the Bible means by *justice* and compare that with the idea of social justice as the term is commonly used today.

Where Does This Unquestioned Answer Come From?

The dueling protest signs tell a story of pain and division. On one side of the street, protesters carry signs saying, "Homelessness is not a crime!" On the other side, counterprotesters wave signs proclaiming, "No homeless shelter here!" Every conflict is painted in stark contrast: "No borders, no walls!" versus "Build the wall nice and tall!" And "Thoughts and prayers won't solve the gun problem!" versus "Disarming me will not protect me!"

Is there any biblical guidance for today's contentious issues? In September 2018 a racially diverse group of evangelical pastors, ranging in age from thirty to nearly eighty, released a "Statement on Social Justice and the Gospel" proclaiming, "We are deeply concerned that values borrowed from secular culture are currently undermining Scripture in the areas of race and ethnicity, manhood and womanhood, and human sexuality."[3]

The liberal Christian activist John Pavlovitz fired back, accusing the signers of being "white, Conservative, old men" who are "rapidly dying dinosaurs approaching extinction" and who are panicked because they are losing control as society becomes "more intelligent, more scientifically aware, more connected across faith traditions and borders." He concluded, "Jesus was a social justice warrior."[4]

Social justice warrior. Few terms are as divisive in today's political climate. Some proudly wear the label to signal their concern for the poor and oppressed. Others see it as a smoke screen for leftist social engineering.

From the Bible we know that God doesn't choose sides in the way we might want him to. Encountering an angel with a drawn sword, the Old Testament warrior Joshua asked, "Are you for us or for our enemies?" The angel replied, "Neither ... but as commander of the army of the LORD I have now come" (Josh. 5:13–14 NIV).

The angel's point is clear. The question is not whether God is on our side but whether we are on his.

What God thinks is made manifest throughout the pages of Scripture. The Bible portrays us—all of us—as criminals who are offered complete pardons by the Judge of the universe and deputized to proclaim God's good news. By the power of the Holy Spirit, we see this messy world for what it is so we can set it right. Redeemed people live differently. The pursuit of justice flows naturally from hearts reconciled to God. William Wilberforce and his Clapham Circle colleagues worked to abolish the slave trade in England. Mother Teresa and the Missionaries of Charity cared for the poor in India. Sojourner Truth and others advocated for the rights of women.

Today Christian organizations such as International Justice Mission and Prison Fellowship advocate for the oppressed. They have secured landmark legislation to fight sex trafficking and reform the criminal justice system. Beyond legislation, volunteers in such organizations give their time and treasure to personally intervene on behalf of those who have been treated unjustly. This is true of thousands of ministries operating at the local, state, and national levels.

Much of what the Bible teaches about justice is expressed in two Hebrew words. *Mishpat* refers to what is needed to restore justice from injustice. *Tzadeqah* is the state of a society in which justice reigns.[5] In his book *Generous Justice*, Pastor Timothy Keller said, "When these two words, *tzadeqah* and *mishpat*, are tied together, as they are over three dozen times, the English expression that best conveys the meaning is 'social justice.'"[6]

Here's the rub. The problem with translating *tzadeqah mishpat* as "social justice" is not that it is a bad interpretation. It's that words convey ideas and ideas have histories. Sadly the term *social justice* no longer conveys what it once meant. Today it's a term held hostage by people with specific political agendas. An Oxford dictionary defines the current meaning of *social justice* as "justice in terms of the distribution of wealth, opportunities, and privileges within a society."[7] In other words, social justice is achieved when society takes wealth, opportunities, and privileges from those who have more and redistributes them to those who have less.[8] We could debate whether this is a wise policy, and it is one that Pastor Keller specifically argued against, but it is clear that what the term implies today differs significantly from the way the Bible speaks of justice.

Some people would push back against my conclusion. "Is Jesus not a prototype for a modern-day social justice warrior?" they ask. "After all, he fed the hungry. He treated women and children as the equals of men. He even conversed with a Samaritan, which wasn't socially acceptable for any respectable Jewish person."

Yes, Jesus acted justly. As we read Scripture, though, we see that Jesus's actions had more than people's immediate needs in mind. Jesus's ministry revealed God's plan for all of history. Care for the poor and oppressed may be the paper on which his ministry was printed, but that's not the point of the narrative.

Worse, mischaracterizing Jesus's ministry plays into the hands of a political agenda with distinctly anti-Christian goals. The concepts behind social justice, as the term is often used today, find their roots in Karl Marx's *Communist Manifesto*. Marx called for a revolution to seize power, wealth, and status from the "haves" and redistribute them to the "have-nots." As an atheist Marx thought justice would be secured only if we "sweep away everything that claims to be supernatural and superhuman."[9]

To be clear, it is wrong for the rich to exploit the poor. It is wrong for companies to glean profits by diverting funds dedicated to worker safety. But how do we make these wrongs right? This debate has taken place in universities and the halls of government for decades. It has also taken place in churches. In the early part of the twentieth century, a New York City pastor named Walter Rauschenbusch published *A Theology for the Social Gospel*, which defined *sin* as "selfishness" and implied that salvation would be achieved by ushering in the kingdom of God through good works that changed society.[10]

Reaction to the social gospel was immediate and intense. Many Christians wanted nothing to do with this new doctrine. They thought that Pastor Rauschenbusch was teaching a false salvation of resolving the world's problems through human goodness rather than biblical repentance.[11]

Speaking for myself, I've become uncomfortable using the term *social justice*, especially when it is tied to Jesus's life and ministry. It has too much baggage. Plus, it's no longer clear what we're talking about when we talk about social justice. But what should replace it? This question drives us back to the heart of what the Bible says about justice in the first place.

What Does the Bible Teach Us about Justice?

The Mosaic Law (also called the Torah) is the earliest source of God's revelation to the Israelites. Newly freed from slavery, the Hebrews needed laws to govern themselves while surrounded by hostile nations and possessing no natural sources of food and water. Survival was at stake. At its heart, the Torah tells the story of how life ought to be lived. It contains profoundly helpful insights into justice, environmental stewardship, property, welfare, criminal law, marriage and divorce, and sex.[12] Rabbis counted 613 laws in the Jewish Bible. Jesus later affirmed that all these laws fall into two categories: loving God and loving our neighbors (Luke 10:26–28). Let's look at both of them.

Loving God

We love God with our all. Deuteronomy 6 contains one passage of the Shema, one of two prayers that Jewish people say every day: "Hear, O Israel: The LORD our God, the LORD is one. You shall love the LORD your God with all your heart and with all your soul and with all your might" (v. 4–5). Everything else flows from this.

We love God because he first loved us (1 John 4:19). We bear God's image (Gen. 1:27). We are human *beings*, not human *doings*. Our worth comes from God, not from our activities. We are distinct and inherently valuable persons regardless of size, age, gender, ethnicity, ability, or intelligence.[13]

Loving Our Neighbors

Since we are all image bearers, loving our neighbors is one of the main ways we express our love for God. Loving our neighbors goes far beyond waving to them from the driveway. It's a practical kind of love that applies to all society. Take, for example, this Mosaic command: "When a man opens a pit, or when a man digs a pit and does not cover it, and an ox or a donkey falls into it, the owner of the pit shall make restoration. He shall give money to its owner, and the dead beast shall be his" (Ex. 21:33–34). In other words, if something you do hurts your neighbor, you must make it right. Such instruction about neighborliness evolved into what we call "tort law": we are obligated to act in a way that won't harm our neighbors' interests.[14]

The Old Testament law also focuses on loving neighbors by restoring the rights of victims. If someone stole an animal, that person was to repay four or five times the value (22:1). If a person lied on a contract or profited by deceiving a neighbor, that person was to repay what was taken and add a fifth to it as compensation (Lev. 6:2–5).

When injustice occurs, it throws the nature of things out of balance. This balance must be restored. That's why justice is often pictured as an old-fashioned scale. Imagine that you're texting while driving and accidentally sideswipe a parked car. In so doing, you have committed at least two injustices. You've harmed the interests of another person, the car's owner, and you've harmed the community by neglecting your civic responsibility to drive carefully. Pretending it didn't happen and sneaking away from the scene would create an even greater injustice. Blaming the car's owner for choosing that particular parking spot doesn't restore justice. Nor does faulting the city for aligning the driving lanes the way it did. The only way to restore justice is to make things right with those whose interests were harmed by your carelessness.

From God's perspective, justice doesn't primarily have to do with the compassion you show others or the anger you feel when you've been mistreated. Biblical justice is based on God's nature. When injustice occurs, the balance must be restored. Justice is a mental concept, but it is very real.

Echoing from the Old Testament's rock-hard justice provisions is a longing for the Messiah. He is the one who ultimately brings good news to the poor, binds up the brokenhearted, proclaims liberty to the captives, and sets the prisoners free (Isa. 61:1–2). Humanity's sin knocked the moral universe out of its orbit, affecting every person and aspect of creation. But through the Messiah, God makes all things new and enables us to become "right-makers."

How Justice Fits into Jesus's Mission

Jesus is the Messiah. That is the testimony of fulfilled prophecy, the rest of Scripture, and the evidence for Jesus's resurrection. Speaking as the Messiah, Jesus said, "I am the way, and the truth, and the life" (John 14:6). It's a threefold claim that helps us see how Jesus's messiahship can resolve the tension we feel over the question of social justice.

First, Jesus claimed to be the way. His disciples would have recognized the term *the way* as the equivalent of the Hebrew word *derek*, which often refers to the overall direction of a person's life.[15] There is a good way to go and a bad way to go. Jesus doesn't just point the way; he *is* the way. His teachings show what redemption looks like lived out. Followers of Jesus seek peace, resolve anger, speak forthrightly, resist retaliation for personal offenses, love their enemies, and give to those in need. The kingdom journey is not about following a set of rules; rather, it's about following a person, who leads us to the God who sees us not as his slaves but as his children (John 1:12).

Jesus also claimed to be the truth. He claimed to fulfill Isaiah's prophecy (Luke 4:17–21). If Jesus is the Messiah, then we need to reexamine the Old Testament prophecies in that light. If the Messiah has come, then deception, abuse, and injustice have lost their power over us. Isaiah 42 says of the Messiah, "He will not grow faint or be discouraged till he has established justice in the earth" (v. 4). Lies don't win the day anymore, because the Messiah knows the truth. The Messiah *is* the truth. His very presence focuses us on God's nature, and he will never give up until everything is made new.

Finally, Jesus claimed to be the life. Through Jesus a life of shalom—wholeness or completeness—becomes possible. Shalom doesn't divide; it multiplies. In shalom we ask, *How can we help one another grow as persons and become more complete image bearers of God?* Shalom doesn't just feed the hungry or rescue the oppressed. It transforms the poor into good stewards who bear fruit. It turns the rescued into rescuers. And it rescues the rescuers from patronizing pride as they realize they are growing and benefiting every bit as much as those they seek to help.

In the end, biblical justice is personal. "The line dividing good and evil cuts through the heart of every human being," said Aleksandr

Solzhenitsyn.[16] We are not the politically pure bringing enlightenment to the masses. Rather, we are the redeemed bearing the good news to others who, like ourselves, are hopelessly lost without it. We love our neighbors not just by avoiding wrongdoing but by setting our minds and hearts to "right doing." The essential question is not "Would Jesus endorse my political and social views?" Instead, we should ask, "What barriers stop me from being like Jesus and living fully for him?"

Don't leave justice at a theoretical level. If you have caused injustice, don't rest until you make it right. If you want to share Jesus's good news, don't just use words. Invest time helping alleviate the pain of injustice others have experienced. Minister to the poor. Sign up for foster care. Fight sex trafficking. Run for city council. Start a neighborhood watch. Make your home a safe place for kids. Care for single moms. Reach out to prisoners.

My wife, Stephanie, and I have been involved in a community center helping single moms and their kids. We have also helped groups such as Save the Storks, which makes it easy for pregnant women to get ultrasounds. Stephanie and her mom love helping with the Night to Shine program, which makes people with special needs feel loved and honored. Privately we've also helped individuals get back on their feet financially and used our home as a refuge for those who've experienced trauma.

From God's perspective, justice isn't something "out there" that can be reached only if we support massive social programs aimed at addressing the root cause. Justice is practical, and it begins with me and with you.

———

Jesus did not come to be a social justice warrior. He came as the Son of God to reconcile us to the Father. Such a great salvation restores our capacity to love God and, in turn, love our neighbors. This doesn't mean you have to be a Christian to pursue justice. But it does mean that true purpose, true peace, and true justice have their source in Jesus, whether we recognize it or not.

Because Jesus is the way, the truth, and the life, we humans can know what justice is, see the truth, and live lives of wholeness and completeness with those around us. It's part of God's grace to humanity. Even those who deny that Jesus is the savior can experience justice.

You don't have to be a wealthy person with lots of free time to do this. Brian Skaret, the attorney who helped restore justice to the people of Juárez, Mexico, told me that his journey began at Summit Ministries when he was just a teenager. There he realized there's this logical progression from what we believe about the creation of the world and whether we need a savior—there's this association between that and the types of issues that we confront in society every single day.[17]

There will always be people who seek to co-opt the desire for justice to advance their political and social agendas. For most of us, though, it's not just about the causes we support. It's about the kinds of conversations we have every day. This is something I learned one summer day outside a cake shop as I approached a group of protesters enraged by a Supreme Court decision.

Discussion Questions

1. What are some injustices that you have witnessed?

2. How has your faith influenced your view of justice?

3. Can biblical justice and social justice be reconciled in today's society? How?

4. How do you see Jesus as the fulfillment of our desire for justice?

8

"It's Not My Place to Judge"

Rediscovering Truth about Judgment

I hadn't been to a protest for a while, and I'd forgotten how much demonstrations reveal about the deep divide we face in our times. Then I got a call about a group called the Gay Army, which intended to protest Jack Phillips's cake shop in Lakewood, Colorado, less than a two-hour drive from Summit Ministries' headquarters.

Jack Phillips is the cake artist who declined to create a custom cake for a same-sex wedding. The Colorado Civil Rights Commission punished him with a fine and required sensitivity training. At the US Supreme Court, the justices ruled seven to two that the commission had overstepped its bounds. Some within the LGBTQ community resented the decision and were up in arms.

Wanting to support Jack and sensing an opportunity to give our Summit students an experience in civic engagement, I asked our team to develop a plan. Our instructors trained the students on the legal issues and other topics surrounding same-sex attraction, and the students role-played how to dialogue with others in a hostile situation. The message to our students was clear: *If you're hoping to simply be entertained, stay home. Everyone who comes should be prepared to engage personally and share Jesus with others.*

On the morning of the protest, more than fifty Summit students and staff traveled to Lakewood. When we arrived at Masterpiece Cakeshop, we found a line of customers stretching down the sidewalk. I went inside and gave Jack a hug. He seemed to be taking the chaos in stride.

Meanwhile the protesters arrived. Having heard they would arrive by the hundreds, we were startled at the tiny group of maybe twenty standing shyly a few yards away.

Along with my friend Ryan, I approached a couple of the protesters. We offered bottles of water, told them our names, asked for their viewpoint, and shared our own. This annoyed an older man standing behind a couple of the demonstrators. He hissed to one of them, "This is how they do it. They're all nice one on one, but in groups they're like *piranhas.*"

Looking directly at Ryan and me, he shouted, "*F— you!*" and turned to walk away. Suddenly he wheeled around and moved in close. "I bet you never talk about *f—ing*, do you?" he spat. "*F—*! I bet that makes your Christian ears burn, *doesn't* it?"

"Not really," Ryan replied calmly.

"We love you," I called out as he strode away and raised his middle finger in reply.

As Ryan and I returned to our chat with the protesters, I noticed Summit students following our cue, offering bottles of water and engaging others in conversation.

This all worked well for a few minutes until a new protester arrived to organize things and get an old-fashioned battle line formed.

With her tiny group arrayed behind her, the newcomer began shouting through a bullhorn: "This whole thing shows me that capitalism has taken a much bigger hold than I imagined. This is about a *cake*, people! We're fighting each other over a *f—ing cake!*"

That was it. As soon as the protester cursed through the bull-horn, the Lakewood police closed in and moved the protesters to a public sidewalk a hundred yards away and out of sight of the cake shop. As they turned to leave, the old man gestured obscenely again and a same-sex couple stopped to share a passionate kiss, hoping our Summit students were watching. But they weren't. They were focused on handing out bottles of water to a group of tattooed, camo-wearing flag-wavers standing across the driveway.

Later as I reflected on the day, I was proud of our Summit students for moving toward the situation rather than away from it. They handled tense conversations with respect and decorum. Still, the situation seemed lose-lose. Nothing was resolved. Both sides saw it as a justice issue. Supporters of Jack Phillips were angry that Jack's business was nearly destroyed while he and his family endured five years of death threats. The protesters had felt bullied over their sexuality, and they blamed Christians. They perceived that Jack and others like him wore religious freedom as a cloak to disguise their hate.

Christianity's general image problem doesn't make the conflict any easier. A few years back, *Time* magazine publicized a poll finding that 87 percent of young nonchurchgoers characterize evangelical Christians as "judgmental."[1] The statistic sent shock waves throughout the church world and propelled the pollster's book *unChristian* onto bestseller lists.

In the years since, much discussion has centered on how Christians come across in the culture. Conflicts like those surrounding Masterpiece Cakeshop bring underlying tensions to the surface. "Jesus would have baked the cake," some say. Others point out that Jesus would say, "Go and sin no more."

Most people don't like conflict or being viewed negatively. So, rather than come across as rude to nonbelievers, many believers repeat the mantra "It's not my place to judge." In support, they reference John 8, the narrative of Jesus intervening on behalf of a woman about to be executed for adultery. "Let him who is without sin among you be the first to throw a stone at her," he said (v. 7). We tell ourselves that Jesus didn't judge and neither should we.

The "no judgment allowed" mind-set is growing in popularity among Christians. A joint Summit Ministries and Barna Group poll found that churchgoing Christians under age forty-five were nearly four times as likely as those over forty-five to strongly believe that "if your beliefs offend someone or hurt their feelings, it is wrong."[2] Does the fact that people find biblical truth offensive mean we should stop proclaiming it? More and more Christians think the answer is yes.

The role of judgment in society and personal relationships relates directly to how we view the world. We need to understand where the "it's not my place to judge" impulse comes from, what the Bible says about truth and moral judgment, and how we can learn to speak the truth in love.

Where Does This Unquestioned Answer Come From?

Obviously, expressing judgments doesn't necessarily make a person judgmental. Good judgment is a virtue. It's what allows us to assess whether others pose a threat, whether they have our best interests in mind, and whether their actions are wise or foolish. Research shows that it takes only a tenth of a second to form a first impression and these quickly formed impressions are consistent with those developed over a longer period.[3]

We use the term *judgmental,* on the other hand, to describe those who easily find fault with others, especially if they do so in an uncaring, ignorant, or bullying way. This describes more and more people in our society. When Senator Ben Sasse and his young son set up a water station at a marathon in Lincoln, Nebraska, protesters gathered across the street and screamed at runners, "It's poison! He wants you to die!"[4] Such vilifications are horrifying but not at all shocking to those who use social media and are accustomed to the "us versus them" narrative. We're told to express tolerance of everyone except, of course, those we view as intolerant.

Regardless of what people outside the church do, there is no place for Christians to demean others. But we also can't escape a simple fact: holding a belief implies that people who believe otherwise are mistaken. For example, Christians believe in an afterlife. Buddhists reject this belief and say that life is a cycle of deaths and rebirths. These two beliefs cannot both be true at the same time (though they could both be false, which is what atheists believe). This disagreement between the two will hang over the relationship of a Christian and a Buddhist, at least if they take their respective beliefs seriously.

Christians who try to avoid judging others often develop one of three responses.

First, some categorize moral statements as opinions rather than facts. "This is what I believe, but it's just my opinion, and yours might be different." But facts and opinions are different things, and we ought to know the difference. Claiming that "Barack Obama was elected president of the United States in 2008" is different from claiming that "medium-rare steak is best." Claiming that moral statements can be only matters of opinion implies that there is no overarching truth or that even if there is, no one could know it.

Second, some try to avoid judging by saying that God himself doesn't judge, so we shouldn't either. When asked a question about gay priests, Pope Francis replied, "Who am I to judge?" He was later asked about his comment and replied, "Mercy is real; it is the first attribute of God."[5] Pope Francis appeared to be referring to God's appearance to Moses, when God proclaimed about himself, "The LORD, the LORD, a God merciful and gracious, slow to anger, and abounding in steadfast love and faithfulness" (Ex. 34:6). This may seem nitpicky, but to say that mercy is first leaves the impression that God's attributes are like items on a list and that he focuses on one by momentarily setting the others aside. And since God is always merciful, the pontiff seems to have been saying, our impression of him as a God of judgment is incorrect. We aren't to judge, because God himself doesn't judge.

If I were to meet Pope Francis, I hope I would have the courage to share my conviction that God doesn't have the multitasking problem that we humans do. His attributes coexist in perfect harmony: God is a merciful judge. Our job as image bearers is to find ways to do what is right with hearts of mercy.

Third, some try to solve the problem of judgment by implying that we aren't allowed to express moral judgments until we ourselves are completely pure. In "Judge Not," Bob Marley sang,

> Don't you look at me so smug …
> Who are you to judge me[6]

Marley is right on one point: it's bad to be a hypocrite. Yet saying "You can't judge until you're perfect" is still a judgment, isn't it? When someone says, "Don't judge," we could respond, "Is it your judgment that I should not judge?" Maybe it's just a trick of how language works, but judgment seems unavoidable. To say "You can't judge, because you can't know ultimate reality" is to claim to know something ultimate about both judgment and reality.

If correct, these three beliefs about moral judgments place us in a catch-22. Moral judgments are just opinions; not even God makes them. And even if he did, we shouldn't follow suit unless we're perfect. The way out of the dilemma is through the teachings of Jesus himself. Shortly after saying "Let him who is without sin among you be the first to throw a stone at her" (John 8:7), Jesus told his followers, "If you abide in my word, you are truly my disciples, and you will know the truth, and the truth will set you free" (vv. 31–32). That's what we need: truth and freedom. But how do we get it?

Is There Such a Thing as Truth?

Respected scholars J. P. Moreland and Garrett DeWeese said that for us to know any one thing, the following three things are required. First, we must have a *belief*—an idea about reality. Second, our belief must be *true*, which means it corresponds to reality. True beliefs are ideas that reflect the way things really are. But holding a true belief still isn't quite enough, because we might just have a hunch about it or take a lucky guess. We also require a third thing—a *warrant* for our beliefs. We need to be able to justify them.[7]

Justified true belief. That's what we're shooting for. We can develop justified true beliefs through reason, observation, experience, introspection, or authority. For example, I am justified in believing that I'm angry or happy through introspection, by looking inside myself. I am justified in believing that my office chair is sturdy because my experience has shown it has always held me up. When I have justified true beliefs, then I can say I *know* they are true.

Christianity claims that the Bible accurately describes the contours of the world as it actually exists. Further, Christianity says this truth is observable by anyone who is capable of understanding and who is not so stubborn as to refuse to see it. It is justifiably believed.

When Christians say they know their faith is true, they're saying they have a belief that corresponds to reality and is justified by reason, observation, experience, and so forth. If the Bible's description of a loving, wise, just, personal, creative God is based on reality, then what this God says about right and wrong must also be based on reality. The Bible's moral commands—such as "You shall not murder" (Ex. 20:13) and "You shall not bear false witness" (v. 16)—are based on reality.

If the Bible's moral teachings are rooted in reality, then they won't change based on the passage of time or our circumstances or because we stop liking them. In this sense, they are universal.

Belief in universal morals corresponds to and explains what we know to be true about the world. Philosopher Richard H. Beis collected a fascinating list of morals that seem to be accepted in every culture studied by anthropologists. Here is a partial list:

- prohibition of murder or maiming without justification
- prohibition of lying, at least in certain areas such as oaths
- right to own property such as land, clothing, tools, and so on
- economic justice: reciprocity and restitution
- preference of common good over individual good

- demand for cooperation within the group
- sexual restrictions[8]
- reciprocal duties between children and parents: parents care for and train children; children respect, obey, and care for parents in old age
- loyalty to one's social unit (family, tribe, country)
- provision for the poor and unfortunate
- prohibition of theft
- prevention of violence within in-groups
- obligation to keep promises
- obedience to leaders
- respect for the dead and disposal of human remains in some traditional and ritualistic fashion
- desire for and priority of immaterial goods (knowledge, values, etc.)
- obligation to be a good mother
- recognition of courage as a virtue
- identification of justice as an obligation[9]

These morals are widespread, but that's not what makes them true. They are widespread *because* they are true. They are not sensible because they work so well—they work so well because they are sensible. They are justified true beliefs based on reality.

So why do we face so much disagreement and confusion? It's not because God is unclear about who he is and what he wants. It is because God has communicated clearly but we have *rebelled*. "All have sinned and fall short of the glory of God" (Rom. 3:23).

Of course, many people object to the very idea that we can know the truth and live differently as a result. Their objections are often expressed through parables like the one featuring blind men touching an elephant: One man handles the tail and exclaims that an elephant is like a rope. Another grasps a leg and describes the elephant as a tree trunk. A third feels the tusk and says the animal is similar to a spear, and so on. Since each feels only a small portion of the whole elephant, the men describe their experiences differently. Only by putting their observations together can they arrive at a complete picture of the elephant.

In other words, we think we are right only because we don't see the big picture. If we fail to admit this, we show ourselves to be intolerant people who are uninterested in reality, peace, and harmony. But the elephant example assumes that the elephant really exists, as does someone—the person telling the story, perhaps—who knows the elephant well enough to see that each blind man has only a partial interpretation.

The heart of Christianity's claim is that someone exists who is not blind, who has complete knowledge, and who has revealed some of this knowledge to us. The Bible is the record of God's creation and his plan for redemption through Jesus Christ. It describes Jesus as the true and living way (John 14:6). He is the key to reality itself (Col. 1:16–17). So, while humans are fallen creatures and cannot know the truth *exhaustively*, Christianity says we can know *truly* what God has revealed.

So how do we communicate this truth without coming across as judgmental know-it-alls?

How to Communicate Truth without Being Judgmental

We naturally want to be at peace with people, even those with whom we strongly disagree. These six actions and attitudes can help.

Trust God

Trusting God means surrendering the outcome to him. You don't need to prevail in a discussion in order for God to accomplish what he wants. It's okay to say something like "This is a big issue, and I'm glad we're taking it seriously. Since it might take a while, I want you to know I'm not in a hurry to get the conversation over with."

Be Humble

Calling for humility doesn't mean God's truth is up for debate. Rather, humility shows openness and a willingness to converse in the hope that God will grant people repentance and lead them to the truth (2 Tim. 2:24–26). Without being dangerously wishy-washy, we can be honest about our own struggles by beginning, "I am a fallen creature, so my ability to reason is far from perfect. But here is what I understand to be true …"

Dialogue Jesus's Way

Our world is filled with propaganda that doesn't persuade people so much as it shuts them down using shame or fear.[10] As the French philosopher Jacques Ellul put it, "Propaganda ceases where simple dialogue begins."[11] A real discussion can begin as easily as by saying, "If you're like me, I would guess you have genuine doubts. I'd like to hear them." As we ask questions, we need to stay focused on living for the good of others (Matt. 20:28) and treating them the way we wish to be treated (Luke 6:31).

Ask Thoughtful Questions

Good questions help us get to know others and gather information about what they believe.[12] Questions display an interest in them, educate us on their perspectives, and allow us to tailor conversations to their needs and interests. Consider questions like these:

1. *"What do you mean by that?"* Be sure you're talking about the same thing by asking for clarification on the key terms. If someone says, "That's not true for me," you want to ask, "What do you mean by 'truth'?"

2. *"How do you know that?"* When someone makes a claim, it isn't true just because the person believes it. Press for justification by asking, "How do you know that?" For example, if someone says, "No one can really know the truth," ask, "How do you know that is a true belief?"

3. *"Can you help me understand?"* Take the conversation to the next level by going on the offensive without *being* offensive. For example, "You say that Christians are judgmental hypocrites. Can you help me understand more about that?"

4. *"How did you come to that conclusion?"* People don't just start believing things. They arrive there through experience and

observation. Find out more about the nature of their beliefs by asking for their stories.

5. *"Can I take some time to think about it?"* Just because someone demands an answer right away does not mean we are obligated to give one. Once we understand the other person's point of view, we can work to formulate a response later, on our own, when the pressure is off.

Listen

Communication research has shown that the deepest change doesn't happen because of how clever, convincing, and trustworthy our case is. It happens because people have the time and space they need to see the truth.[13] Listening is the most persuasive thing you can do, and it starts with a simple statement: "Tell me more about that." Nothing says "I'm listening!" as clearly as a question that honestly solicits further communication and thinking.

Get to the Root

My brother, Scott, who is a longtime pastor, once told me a secret about the nature of conflict: "What it's about is never what it's about." There's a lot more below the surface of what people say. Christian apologist Frank Turek often asks a question similar to this: "If I could prove to you beyond a shadow of a doubt that Christianity is true, would you become a believer?"[14] We could even include "I'm not saying that I can—I'm just wanting to understand what your real objection is."

Facing controversial issues often throws Christians into confusion. We feel pressure to be clever on command. It takes a lot of knowledge and skill to be quick on your feet. Be curious, ask thoughtful questions, and then go study some more and return with more questions.

———

If everything we've talked about in this chapter is true, then it would be dismissive to say "It's not my place to judge." Using this unquestioned answer cuts vital conversations short just when they're becoming meaningful. Instead, we ought to ask questions that display curiosity and friendly determination. If we do this humbly, people will be able to see through our faults and focus on the truth.

God's truth is not up for debate. God's nature is revealed in Scripture, and he means for us to know what is true. Jesus claimed to be the only way to heaven (John 14:6). It's an exclusive claim—no doubt about it. Some think that this fact alone makes it untrue. But to say "It can't be true because it is exclusive" is to claim to know another truth. Why is *that* a justified true belief? The only way you'll find out why people believe as they do is to ask questions.

Christianity recognizes that other religions have discovered some truths. Biblical Christianity, however, is the best source for true knowledge about God—knowledge that allows us to assess claims about his existence and what he requires of us.

Yes, unfortunately some Christians come across as judgmental hypocrites. But it's wrong to think that all Christians are intolerant because *some* behave badly. That's like saying Mozart is a bad

composer because a nine-year-old piano student plays his composi-
tions poorly. For those who've never heard anything but a poor
performance of Mozart, it's natural to assume that he was an untal-
ented composer or that his music is too difficult to be performed.

It's up to the church to show the world that God is good and that
we can know him and be reconciled to him. As Pastor Tony Evans
put it, "To be a part of the church of Jesus Christ, as Jesus defined it,
is to be a part of a spiritual legislative body tasked to enact heaven's
viewpoint in hell's society."[15]

The next time you're tempted to fall back on the unquestioned
answer "It's not my place to judge," resist. Ask; don't just tell. Allow
God to work through you to strongly show himself to others.

Of course, all of this assumes that what is happening in our
world really matters. Here are questions a lot of people ask: Is there
any point to what is happening here on this planet? Isn't the important stuff in the spiritual world? These are questions I asked while
riding in a car across California with a hippie, and I found myself
surprised at what I learned.

Discussion Questions

1. Are Christians called to judge others? If so, how can we do this
lovingly?

2. Have you ever shied away from a confrontation by using this
cliché? What was the confrontation?

3. When have you felt judged? How did that experience make you feel? How did you respond?

4. What tactic would you like to try in your next challenging interaction?

9

"This World Has Nothing for Me"

Rediscovering Truth about the World

Excitement coursed through my veins as I gazed out the airplane window. The scenery below shifted from rocky desert to gently sloping hills with the ocean beyond. At twenty-three I was seeing California for the first time.

Like most kids who grew up in the eighties, I idealized California, especially the way I imagined the Golden State to have been in the sixties. I looked forward to attending a service at a church that had been at the epicenter of the Jesus movement. Real, live hippies! That was something I hadn't seen at the preppy university I attended at the time.

My host had been part of this movement of people who gave their lives to Christ in the late 1960s and called themselves "Jesus people." She was a genuine flower child—by then with grown children—and she still retained a spunky, slightly rebellious attitude. As I rode with her to her family's home, I drank in the sights—sunshine, palm trees, and tons of traffic—and peppered her with questions about the Jesus movement.

"In the sixties, people felt like the world was going to end soon, so we figured we should just live for the day," she told me. "Jesus people fit right into that message. We're only visiting this planet, right? The rapture could happen at any moment. Let's get turned on to Jesus and win souls."

"But what if Jesus isn't coming back soon?" I challenged. "What if there is no such thing as a rapture?"

My host nearly drove off the road. Knuckles white on the steering wheel, she turned to me and said, "There has to be a rapture coming. That's the whole reason I came to Jesus."

I could see I had crossed a line, and I didn't want to be *that* guy, so I changed the subject. Yet I still wondered, *Is the world really going to end soon? If so, shouldn't we all quit our jobs so we can win souls without distraction?*

As I write this, the sixties have been over for half a century. While part of me admires the sheer enthusiasm of the Jesus people and the Jesus movement, another part wonders what kind of difference they might have made if, fifty years ago, they had embraced a more long-term focus. Many of our society's problems are as bad as they were then, and some are much worse. Of course, people usually do the best with what they know at the time. Is it fair to have expected these enthusiastic young hippies to have done more? Were they even responsible for influencing the larger culture? Are we?

In the past, Christians dug in for the long haul. William Wilberforce and his friends worked for forty-three years before slavery was abolished in the British Empire. Europe's great cathedrals often took over one hundred years to build. Imagine working on a building project started by your great-great-grandfather!

But maybe we no longer have that luxury. Perhaps the idea of planting things that won't bear fruit during our lifetimes is made irrelevant by the urgency of today's challenges. I relate to this sense of urgency. As a child it chilled me—even scared me—when I heard songs like Larry Norman's "I Wish We'd All Been Ready":

> There's no time to change your mind;
> The Son has come and you've been left behind.[1]

When I listened to this song recently, I remembered my childhood terror when I was separated from my parents in a large convention hall. I hated being left behind for five minutes, not to mention the thought of suffering years of tribulation at the hands of the Antichrist. I prayed over and over, *God, please don't leave me behind even though I am a bad boy.*

For the first couple of years after I gave my life to Christ, that sense of urgency left me bewildered about what to do with my life. I wanted to get a doctoral degree but knew it would take at least five years. I wanted to get married, but wouldn't it be selfish to spend my time and energy on one person when the whole world needed Jesus? Developing a career would take decades. If the world is going to pass away, why spend time fixing up a junkyard?[2]

Given my academic bent, I grappled with my questions about the future by going down the rabbit hole of eschatology—the theological study of the end times. I studied premillennial viewpoints that anticipated the imminent rapture of the church and a thousand-year reign of Christ. I studied amillennialism, which said that the thousand-year reign of Christ was figurative, not a literal number of years. I studied the postmillennial viewpoint, which said that Christ will return to claim his throne once we've accomplished the Great Commission.

As I met various Christian leaders, I queried them about their own end-times views. The late Christian theologian Norman Geisler put me in my place.

"Dr. Geisler," I said, "are you premillennial, amillennial, or postmillennial?"

"I'm panmillennial," he said, straight faced.

"Panmillennial?" I pressed. "I haven't heard of that."

With a wry grin, Geisler replied, "I believe it will all pan out in the end."

Dr. Geisler's kidding helped me see that while end-times questions are important, the life of this world is something Jesus cares about very much. It's worth investing in for the long haul.

This generation of young adults is being deeply damaged by a short-term mind-set. They have everything that can be gotten quickly and little worth keeping for a lifetime. I recently came across a heartbreaking internet discussion thread that put words to what I've heard from many students over the years: "There is nothing for me in this world.... I spend basically all my times playing games and feeling empty. I have contemplated suicide pretty much every day for at least the past 8 years and I feel like I may be nearing the point where I finally have the [blank] to do it."[3] Several people responded compassionately to that post, but the thread ended three years ago. I don't know the rest of the story. I pray the writer found something to live for.

Meanwhile I'm growing more and more uncomfortable singing words like "This world has nothing for me; I will follow you"[4] or "This world has nothing for me ... and nothing that I need."[5] I suspect there is a bigger story to be told about God's engagement in his creation. In the pages ahead, we'll explore the unquestioned answer "This world has nothing for me" to see what the Bible says and how we might reset our thinking about this cliché.

Where Does This Unquestioned Answer Come From?

A car in my eclectic new age neighborhood sports a bumper sticker that says, "We are not physical beings having a spiritual experience; we are spiritual beings having a physical experience." According to this way of thinking, the physical world either is an illusion or is irrelevant to what is important.

Many Christians find this view compelling and even believe it to be biblical. This world is not our home. Jesus taught his followers that the world hated him and will hate us as well (John 15:18–21).

"Foxes have holes, and birds of the air have nests, but the Son of Man has nowhere to lay his head," Jesus said (Matt. 8:20).

In his first letter to the Corinthians, Paul wrote that we do not have "the spirit of the world" and that "the wisdom of this world is folly with God" (2:12; 3:19). In his second he wrote, "We would rather be away from the body and at home with the Lord" (5:8).

The apostle John warned, "Do not love the world or the things in the world. If anyone loves the world, the love of the Father is not in him" (1 John 2:15). The apostle James piled this on: "Whoever wishes to be a friend of the world makes himself an enemy of God" (James 4:4).

It's not hard to imagine why so many early Christians longed to leave this world behind. Their lives were full of toil, poverty, disease, and sadistic rulers. The religious and political leaders of Jesus' day conspired to kill him through crucifixion, a form of execution exquisitely designed to maximize both suffering and humiliation. Countless Jesus followers died horrible deaths. No wonder "Come, Lord Jesus!" was the prayer on the lips of many (Rev. 22:20).

It was against this backdrop of human misery that the religious movement of gnosticism arose in the first and second centuries. Gnosticism taught that a lesser god known as the Demiurge was responsible for creating the material world, which is evil.[6] To gnostics, salvation comes through secret knowledge—*gnosis*—about how the spirit can escape the bondage of the physical body and the material world. The spirit was seen as the true person. Bodies just slow us down.[7]

With the ever-present threat of persecution, some early Christians found gnosticism compelling, with its emphasis on the spiritual rather than material world. Yet the early church fathers vigorously opposed it as heresy. In response to gnosticism, Irenaeus of Lyons (c. AD 130–200) stressed God's unity and the goodness of the created world.[8] The Apostles' Creed—which focuses on God as the creator and Christ as the redeemer who entered creation itself—was, in its initial form, written as a line-by-line argument against heresies, including gnosticism.[9]

Christianity isn't gnostic. Christians shouldn't think that the spiritual and material worlds have nothing to do with each other. But Christians' hesitation to fully involve themselves in the life of the world has opened the door to a completely secular interpretation of philosophy, politics, economics, and history.[10] This failure has also convinced many influencers that Christianity has nothing important to say about the world around us. Georgetown University professor Jacques Berlinerblau contrasted his secular beliefs with those of religious people by saying, "The secularish are here-and-now people. They live for this world, not for the next."[11] Professor Berlinerblau teaches his students—many of whom have become national leaders—that worldviews focused on spiritual things are simply not up to the task of governing in a complex, religiously pluralistic society.

Many people who reject a Christian worldview hope that Christians will continue to ignore the world around them, leaving secularist leaders to rule it however they wish. When Christians do get involved, such leaders find it very irritating. One of them once said, "Things have come to a pretty pass when religion is allowed to invade public life." The archaic phrase *pretty pass* probably clued you in to the fact that this was said a long time ago. It was. Two hundred years ago, by Lord Melbourne, a British parliamentarian opposing

William Wilberforce's efforts to abolish slavery.[12] Lord Melbourne's sentiment is offered today, though, in the halls of power and the ivy-covered edifices of our most prestigious universities. If Christians stay silent, though, who will bring the Bible's powerful, compassionate solutions into the public square?

Yet many Christians hesitate. They think, *If the world is soon coming to an end, then don't do anything more for this world than is absolutely necessary to get people to make decisions for Christ so they can go to heaven when they die.* Is this how we should think?

What Does the Bible Say about the Material World?

As we've seen, the idea that the material world is evil is a gnostic worldview, not a Christian one. God called creation "very good" (Gen. 1:31) and sent his Son into the physical world to redeem it. Christ is not outside culture or above it. He entered culture to transform it. But is this transformation short term or long term— or both?

We find a clue to how God thinks about culture in the counsel of the Old Testament prophet Jeremiah to Jewish exiles living in Babylon: "Build houses and live in them; plant gardens and eat their produce. Take wives and have sons and daughters; take wives for your sons, and give your daughters in marriage, that they may bear sons and daughters; multiply there, and do not decrease. But seek the welfare of the city where I have sent you into exile, and pray to the LORD on its behalf, for in its welfare you will find your welfare" (Jer. 29:5–7).

The word translated "welfare" is *shalom*, a term we encountered in a previous chapter. A person focused on shalom seeks the good of every person in every relationship.

The heart of the gospel is that God provides shalom and shows us how to offer it to others. Shalom moves people from deformation to reformation, from wasting away to flourishing, from poverty to prosperity, from disorder to order, from injustice to justice, from ignorance to knowledge, and from sickness to health.

The context of Jeremiah 29 is important. Prior to Jeremiah's letter, the Babylonian exiles had been advised to keep their bags packed—soon God was going to whisk them away. Not only did Jeremiah contradict that advice, but he also called the prophet who said it a liar (28:1–15). Your exile will be a long one, Jeremiah said. Settle in and raise families. If you want to prosper, seek the prosperity of those around you.

In short, shalom-focused people aren't headed for the exit. They engage rather than escape. Even when they're in exile, they're determined to keep the "very-good-ness" of God's creative work on full display. This does not minimize the importance of personal salvation. Rather, it highlights it. Once we're saved, God does not instantly beam us up to heaven. He instructs us in what he wants us to do until it's time to go home.

God cared so much about this world that he sent Jesus, who said, "Go therefore and make disciples of all nations … teaching them to observe all that I have commanded you. And behold, I am with you always, to the end of the age" (Matt. 28:19–20). Through his death and resurrection, Jesus has brought God's peace to us, and he now commands us to teach everyone in the world to obey him in every area in which he has authority—which Jesus claims over every area of life. It's time to armor up in God's power and stand for what he is for and against everything he is against. Ephesians 6:10–12 tells believers to take their stand "against the cosmic powers over this present darkness, against the spiritual forces of evil in the heavenly places." When the tide turns toward evil, Paul told his hearers, "Stand firm" (v. 13).

This work will likely not end during our lifetimes. That's okay, because it's not about us anyway. It's about God and what he is doing.

What Must We Do Now?

The heavens and earth will pass away (2 Pet. 3:10). My former-hippie friend was speaking biblically about that as we rode from the airport on that balmy Southern California day.

And I understand her reluctance to put down roots and be an influencer here and now. The world worships its ability to draw a crowd or muster political power, because that's all it's got. There is nothing higher than the ability to make people do what you want. Christians sometimes feel they have to give in to this temptation or withdraw completely. Answering this confusion, the Bible gives us a profound option: we can be *in* the world but not *of* it. Here are four ways to do that.

Cultivate a Conversation-Friendly Explanation of the Gospel

As we've seen in previous chapters, asking questions is the most natural way to engage people with the truth. Try these:

- Are you interested in spiritual things?
- In what ways would you most like to grow spiritually?
- What do you think about Jesus?
- Has anyone ever explained to you what Jesus's message is all about?

If the person seems interested, ask, "Could I give you the CliffsNotes version?" The campus ministry InterVarsity Christian Fellowship distills the gospel message into four points:

- The world and all that's in it were designed for good.
- We—and the world—were damaged by evil.
- Jesus came to restore the world and everything in it to what God intended.
- Jesus invites us to join him and his community in healing the world.[13]

InterVarsity's evangelism.intervarsity.org website offers resources to share these points, including a smartphone app.

If you carry a Bible in your backpack or briefcase, mark these four gospel passages to share:

- *John 1:9–13.* Jesus is the true light, and those who come to him can become children of God.
- *John 5:24.* Jesus can give us eternal life.

- *Romans 3:23–24.* We have all sinned, but we have grace through Jesus.
- *Romans 10:9.* Acknowledge that Jesus is the risen Lord, and you will be saved.

Change Our Time Frame

Focusing on things of eternal value is not the same as ignoring things of temporal value. We can see this by looking at two common Greek words for "time" in the New Testament. One is *chronos*, which refers to *clock* time, and the other is *kairos*, which often refers to *opportunity* time. In this sense, *kairos* cannot be measured; it is always now. Make the best use of the *kairos*, the apostle Paul wrote (Eph. 5:16). In God's economy, temporal minutes are valuable because they create potential moments of eternal significance. Things that pay off decades from now are important. Things that immediately pay off are important too. It's not about *chronos*; it's about *kairos*. Instead of asking, "What can we do quickly?" we should ask, "Where are the best opportunities to highlight what is good, fix what is broken, and stand against the millennia-long effects of evil?"

Making the most of every opportunity is something that applies even to things like "soul winning." I absolutely do not want anyone to face eternity without Christ. But if our souls are everything about us that is not physical—hopes and dreams, victories and ideas, loves and likes—finding what returns energy to us and makes us feel more alive is a vital part of our souls' development.

Develop Our Skill at Communicating God's Truth

Steve Garber, a Christian professor and Summit Ministries speaker, told a story about meeting some musicians who were writing music primarily for a Christian audience. He asked, "If all truth is God's truth, should we be able to write songs in words that speak the truest truths of the universe in language the *whole world* can understand?" Of course! And we should be able to design buildings that everyone in the world can appreciate and use. We should be able to assemble labs that pursue fascinating breakthroughs. If all authority really does belong to Jesus, is there any area of life that cannot be pursued with life-giving shalom?

Consider this example. Indian teacher Krishna Mohan Bannerjee converted to Christianity in 1832 through the mentorship of a British missionary. Bannerjee wrote an Indian adaptation of the *Encyclopaedia Britannica*. At the time, India was a lost culture, practicing a caste system, polygamy, idolatry, child marriage, and *sati*, the practice of burning a woman alive on the funeral pyre of her husband.

Yet Bannerjee understood that a culture that had developed for thousands of years wasn't going to change overnight. Bannerjee sensed that to shape what people in India thought about, he needed to write an encyclopedia (a dictionary, which shapes how people use language to think, had already been written by missionary William Carey). In his encyclopedia, Bannerjee gave voice to how a traditional Hindu way of thinking would lift up human rights and equality.[14] Over time Bannerjee's work changed centuries of thinking.

Bannerjee's project reshaped a nation, but it took time. He didn't assume India had to change immediately. Like a skillful painter, he used nuance and detail to reveal truth in a way that Indians hadn't grasped before. They didn't need to learn a new cultural language in order to understand God. They needed someone to translate God's nature into a cultural language they already knew.

We can do the same thing in our communities. When we pay attention to people's greatest hopes and dreams, their deepest fears and disappointments, we learn how to give voice to the truth every person longs to hear.

Have Hope

The story behind a famous Christmas carol illustrates why we should have hope and how to express it. "I Heard the Bells" was composed Christmas Day 1863 by the beloved American poet Henry Wadsworth Longfellow in Cambridge, Massachusetts. Most people have heard the first verse:

> I heard the bells on Christmas Day
> Their old, familiar carols play,
> And wild and sweet
> The words repeat
> Of peace on earth, good-will to men![15]

Beneath these beautiful lyrics, however, lies a story of a broken man struggling to hold on to his belief in God and humanity. Longfellow had suffered through the death of his first wife and his daughter. Happily, he had found joy again in his marriage to Frances Appleton. But in 1861 tragedy struck again. Frances was melting wax to seal a snip of her daughter's hair in an envelope when her dress caught on fire. Despite her husband's attempts to save her, she died of her horrible injuries.[16]

Adding to personal tragedy, the Northern and Southern armies were at that time locked in vicious combat in which hundreds of thousands of Americans had been killed and maimed. The nation that Abraham Lincoln had called "the last best hope of earth"[17] seemed to be wading in rivers of blood as the slaughter pitted neighbor against neighbor, brother against brother.

Utter loneliness. Hopelessness. Longfellow expressed his sorrow in the sixth verse:

> And in despair I bowed my head;
> "There is no peace on earth," I said;
> "For hate is strong,
> And mocks the song
> Of peace on earth, good-will to men!"[18]

Can you identify with that feeling? We long for things to be right side up in this upside-down world, yet despair seems to be our lot.

The Bible offers one fact—one hope—in a world like this: Christ has risen. The late Catholic thinker Richard John Neuhaus put it beautifully: "We have not the right to despair, for despair is a sin. And finally, we have not the reason to despair, quite simply because Christ has risen. And this is the strength of a Christian world view, the strength of the Christian way of telling the story of the world:

it has no illusions about it. All the other stories are built upon delusions, vain dreams, and utopias."[19]

Revelation 21:3 says, "Behold, the dwelling place of God is with man. He will dwell with them, and they will be his people, and God himself will be with them as their God." God is making all things new (v. 5). This is a hope worth holding and worth proclaiming.

Longfellow gave voice to his despair, but he didn't stop there. With hope rising, he wrote,

> Then pealed the bells more loud and deep:
> "God is not dead; nor doth he sleep!
> The Wrong shall fail,
> The Right prevail,
> With peace on earth, good-will to men!"[20]

This is hope—that God is alive and awake … that he stepped into his own creation, entering the world stage as a helpless baby … that Immanuel, God with us, lived among us and willingly gave himself over to death on the cross, paying the penalty for our sin … that he was resurrected, overcoming death … and that he promises life of the ages to all with ears to hear.

———

We are sojourners on this planet—no doubt. Was my hippie friend right about Jesus coming back soon? I hope so. I also hope that he'll find us hard at work on things that would have yielded fruit for generations had he tarried.

In Christ all things are being made new. The relationships so violently ruptured in the fall can be restored. The walls can be repaired. The ancient paths can be cleared of brush and followed once again. We can experience refreshing and proclaim it to our children and our children's children and our children's children's children until God tells us to stop.

But there's one more unquestioned answer that stands in the way of fully embracing God's plan for this world. It's one that paints a happy face on painful questions: Is God truly good? Does he have our best intentions at heart? These are questions I've dealt with often in my life as a Christian, most recently as I watched the person I love most in this world start to slip away.

Discussion Questions

1. In what ways have you been tempted to ignore the challenges of this world and focus on only heaven instead?

2. What is our responsibility for engaging and changing our world to bring about shalom?

3. How do you see God currently redeeming the world?

4. How can you make the most of each opportunity (*kairos*) you have?

"God Is Good All the Time— All the Time God Is Good"

Rediscovering Truth about God's Goodness

I placed my hand gently on my wife's resting form. I prayed, *Father, she is in such pain and cannot go on like this. If you want to take her, I will be heartbroken. But I will worship you.*

While Stephanie tried to rest, I slipped out of the room and met the duty nurse reviewing her chart. "Thank you," I managed.

"Of course. You're welcome."

"What I mean to say is," I mumbled, my throat thick, "I know you have a lot of patients you're caring for. But to me this one patient is everything."

"We will take good care of her, Mr. Myers. I promise," said the nurse reassuringly. "I hope you'll get some rest."

I shuffled away, trying not to glance in the other rooms lining the hallway of the stroke ward. My thoughts wandered to Stephanie's journey as a spirited survivor who had come to Christ as an aspiring fashion model with a drug problem. The decades since have held many trials, but she has grown strong and shares the love of Jesus with everyone she meets.

When we were introduced, it was a couple of years after the loss of my marriage. As I navigated single parenthood and led a growing ministry, Stephanie became a faithful friend and bold prayer warrior. Three years later, we were married in a fairy-tale wedding with my two sons and two of Stephanie's close friends at our sides. Our pastor opened the ceremony by quoting from George Herbert's poem "The Flower":

> Who would have thought my shrivel'd heart
> Could have recovered greenness?[1]

Our married life together seemed like a dream. We traveled and remodeled a home to host guests and provide a refuge for hurting people. One hundred and sixteen days after our wedding, though, Stephanie woke me early one morning.

"Sweetie," she said, her voice edged with panic, "I have a terrible headache." Something was seriously wrong.

The next two weeks were filled with emergency room visits, hospital stays, batteries of tests, and consultations with nine doctors. Alarm grew as Stephanie lost the strength to stand on her own and found it difficult to form thoughts. Her fingers no longer obeyed her brain, and seizures came several times a day.

One day as I sat beside her in the hospital, she fumbled with her phone. Seeing the puzzled look on her face, I asked, "What's wrong?"

A tear of frustration slid down her cheek. "I forgot how to send a text," she said helplessly.

My heart felt as if it were coming apart cell by cell. *God, we have been through so much heartache, but you gave us the strength to go on. We are serving you. We are so happy. Why this? Why now?*

Behind us the door opened and in walked a youthful-looking man with shaggy hair and a 1970s-style ski sweater. He introduced himself as the neurologist. "I think we've figured out what happened," he said. "It's a very rare kind of stroke, only five out of every million cases."

"Five in a million? So you're saying you have proof that Stephanie is very, very special," I said, glancing over to see whether my lame attempt at humor had earned a smile. It had.

The doctor looked up. "In all seriousness, untreated, this condition has a 48 percent mortality rate. You've dodged a bullet so far."

"What do you mean 'so far'?" I asked, my cobwebbed mind clearing.

The doctor sighed. "We don't know what will happen now. Almost no one on our team has seen this before. There's very little research. I'm sorry I can't tell you more."

Maybe you've had surreal moments like this. You're minding your own business and suddenly find yourself splayed out awkwardly on life's pavement. A loved one is gone. Your career path isn't working out. The sting of betrayal won't subside. Health is failing. A child reveals a hidden, shocking secret.

At such times, chipper social media posts mock us. Television commercials intended to be heartwarming are heartbreaking. The bad news amplifies until we can hear nothing else.

Where are you, God? we ask, trying to swallow our growing suspicion.

Seventy percent of youth group graduates admit they had doubts about God in high school.[2] I used to think that angry atheists caused this. Skeptics stir the pot, certainly, but not as much as you might think. Most struggling people don't question God's *God-ness*—they question his *goodness*.

As I revealed in my book *The Secret Battle of Ideas about God,* I've been there. In such seasons, even going to church can be painful. One day, lost in grief, I listened as a minister exulted, "God is good!" The congregation replied enthusiastically, "All the time!" Then he echoed, "All the time …" And the shouts rang back: "God is good!"

It's a popular call and response, begun by worship leader Don Moen through a song titled "God Is Good All the Time," written as a joyous affirmation of God's goodness. Most of the time its truth washes over me and fills my soul.

That Sunday, though, I squirmed in my seat. *What is happening in the hearts of those around me?* I wondered. *Are they proclaiming God's goodness despite their pain, or are they expressing thanks for a trouble-free week? Or maybe they're barely holding it together, hoping those words will come true. Or secretly concluding, "Nope. God is not good, at least not to me."*

God is good all the time—all the time God is good. That proclamation is an unquestioned answer not because it is theologically suspect—it isn't—but because it risks sounding naive and self-centered at the very moment when our culture is crying out for the gospel's profound answer to its hurts.

Where Does This Unquestioned Answer Come From?

For non-Christians, suffering is a harsh reality to be avoided at all costs. Some religions ignore or deflect the problem of evil and suffering, but Christianity does not. Christians are sometimes called to plunge joyously into suffering in obedience to God (Acts 6:8—7:60; Heb. 12:7–11). Yet the prophet Jeremiah moaned, "Why does the way of the wicked prosper? Why do all who are treacherous thrive?" (Jer. 12:1). In Psalm 13 David cried out, "How long must I take counsel in my soul and have sorrow in my heart all the day?" (v. 2).

Compared with this, the way we talk about God's goodness sometimes betrays a childish obliviousness to the depth of the world's pain. Worse, many take it as self-centered. A chirpy old chorus brightly asserts, "God is so good. God is so good. God is so good. He's so good to me."[3]

"*To me.*" Ah. There it is.

There's not much harm in simple choruses about what God does for us, as far as I can tell. But it's a far cry from how Job responded to his suffering in the Bible. Job didn't deny his predicament or squeeze it down to fit inside the lap-sized box of his preconceptions. Rather, he plainly asked for an answer: *God, I'm sure you have your reasons. If it's not too much trouble, I would like to know what they are.*

It sounds like a reasonable request, but God ignored it. In all his dialogue with Job, God never answered Job's most pressing question: *Why?*

As Job saw it, there were two sorts of evil that caused suffering: natural evil and personal evil. A storm killed his family. Robbers stole his wealth. Natural evil and personal evil.

Natural evil perplexes us. Why does God allow suffering to multiply through drought, disease, flood, and fire? Some parts of nature seem designed to cause suffering. The female tarantula hawk is a wasp that attacks a spider, paralyzing it with a sting and then laying an egg in its body. When the egg hatches, the larva eats the spider's body from the inside out. I'm no fan of spiders, but the Bible strongly encourages ethical treatment of animals as well as people. Isn't God violating his own rules?

Some natural evils defy imagination. I recently read of a birth defect called "harlequin ichthyosis," a genetic mutation causing infants to be born with hard, thick skin that cracks and peels. Sufferers endure agony and face a significantly increased risk of life-threatening infection.

As much as natural evil results in horrible pain, personal evil also causes tremendous suffering. Political scientist R. J. Rummel said that one hundred million or more innocent people were shot, starved, or tortured to death by governments in the twentieth century alone.[4] Every one of those victims was a human being, full of hopes and dreams, a person who loved others and was loved by them.

In our own time, abortion on demand produces a similar kind of holocaust. It targets a specific group—the unborn—and ends lives. As early as six weeks in utero, babies can *feel* it when doctors tear their limbs and crush their skulls. Common abortion procedures are so gruesome that if they happened anywhere but inside a womb, where they remain unseen, the outrage would be immediate and overwhelming.

Nelson Mandela said, "There can be no keener revelation of a society's soul than the way in which it treats its children."[5] If that's true, we need to ask what kind of society we want. The bill always comes due for "victimless" activities, and all too often it is children who pay the price through abandonment, abuse, and addiction.

You don't have to be a Christian to see these evils for what they are and to wonder what they tell us about God. A few years ago, I found myself in a conversation with a successful businessman who somewhat wistfully admitted to being skeptical of Christianity's claims. He confided, "I've suffered a lot. I've caused suffering. I couldn't believe in God, knowing what I know about evil."

I replied, "Sounds like there's quite a story there." I listened as he shared how his struggles with sexual identity had torn his family apart. Though he was wealthy, no amount of money could numb the pain he had endured and caused.

"Christianity has a problem with evil," he said, then explained that either God doesn't care about our suffering, in which case he is not good, or he can't do anything about it, in which case he isn't as powerful as the Bible says.

The businessman's argument is the same one that moved renowned philosopher William Rowe to drop out of Bible college and become an atheist. We don't know everything, he argued, but we know enough to say that pointless suffering indicates there is no God.[6]

So, either God isn't as powerful as the Bible says or, worse, he is fully capable of stopping evil yet looks on passively while his creation suffers. Is there any way out of this dilemma?

What Does the Bible Say?

As the businessman shared his story, I said, "Yes, Christianity does have a problem of evil. But here's something to think about: *every* worldview has a problem of evil."

"Okay," he said, intrigued. "You've got my attention."

"Think about it this way," I replied. "Evil is an unavoidable part of our human experience. Every worldview must explain why we suffer and what we ought to do about it."

Worldviews that deny the existence of anything spiritual contend that the problem *of* evil is that we have a problem *with* evil, I pointed out. There is no higher meaning. Life is painful; then you die. Deal with it.

On the other hand, worldviews that believe only the spiritual world exists contend that suffering is an illusion. In the Bhagavad Gita, part of an Indian epic poem, Lord Krishna responded to Arjuna's grief by saying, "Although you mean well, Arjuna, your sorrow is sheer delusion. Wise men do not grieve for the dead or for the living."[7] Buddhism's approach to suffering runs along a parallel path. Birth, aging, sickness, death, sorrow, pain, grief, and despair can all be overcome by detaching ourselves from the experience of them.[8]

By contrast, the biblical answer to evil and suffering is not *what* but *who*. Through his Son, Jesus Christ, God entered our suffering, conquered death and hell, and is setting the world right.

As I shared these thoughts, I glanced at the businessman and was startled to see a look of tenderness, almost regret, in his eyes.

"What's that look?" I asked.

Shaking his head, he said, "Man, I've never met a Christian who thinks like you." Just then, a friend of his passed by the table where we were standing. "Hey," the businessman called out. "You've got to hear this guy defend Christianity! Ask him a question. Any question."

The newcomer sidled up to the table. "So," he drawled mischievously in his best redneck voice, "what do you think about EE-voh-LOO-tion?" He pounded the table with mock anger, making us laugh. With that, the moment of serious reflection was over. New subject, something lighthearted, but I don't really remember because my mind was wandering back over the terrain of our conversation. Had I said the right thing? What was happening that made the businessman want to quickly change the topic?

Maybe it was that I had started talking about Jesus, although I don't see how I could have done otherwise. Jesus is the ultimate biblical answer to the problem of pain and suffering, and his answer is rooted deeply in everything the Bible teaches about God's nature.

God Is Purposeful and His Understanding Is Unlimited

Knowing all truths and believing no falsehoods, God is perfect in knowledge about the past, present, and future.[9] We humans cannot see the future or fully discern the meaning of the past. Even the present seems like an unsolvable puzzle. Because of his sovereignty, God is not limited in these ways. This is not to say he maintains absolute control, as an engineer running a machine seeks to do. Rather, he is the *ruler* of the universe. He is in charge and has created a world of laws in which we can act in a meaningful way.[10]

God does not dangle us from strings like puppets. Rather, he directs us like in a play.[11] As we make choices, God knows what will happen as a result. He works things out so that when we arrive at the place where our free choices take us, we will see that he has worked in such a way that his good, desired outcome is achieved.[12]

God Created Good

God made everything to be good, the way things ought to be. Not only did he design his creation to be good, he created the very *idea* of good. Evil is not the equal and opposite of good. Rather, it is what deviates from the good. Evil is not a thing in itself; rather, it exists *in* things as a corruption or cancer. Evil is to good what rust is to a car; you know its presence by what ought to be there and isn't anymore. Evil cannot exist without a good it can attack.[13]

Other worldviews find evil difficult to explain because they cannot define what is good in the first place. If only the material world exists, then there is no distinction between what is good and what is evil. We call things we like "good" and things we dislike "evil." But who's to say whether one is better than the other if only the material world exists? On the other hand, some people believe that only the *spiritual* world is real. In this worldview, nothing really exists, so good and evil are just illusions.

We need someone who can see reality from a higher perspective. We need God if we are to understand good.

God Made Us Free

If I program a computer to say "I love you," I know it isn't real love. The computer is doing what I told it to do. God didn't make us to be computers. He made us free. By creating us free, God made evil possible because we had the power to withhold good or act contrary to it.[14] God made a world filled with stones that people could either fashion into sturdy buildings or fling at one another.

God does not take away the freedom that makes it possible for us to do evil. Instead, he willingly withholds his own power so we can be free to perform good actions to counteract evil.[15]

God Directs Us to Take Responsibility

God made us free so we can do what is right. Christianity is not a "see no evil, hear no evil" religion. Moral good is possible in the world God created. We can *know* good and recognize when it is being attacked by evil. We can *do* good that is meaningful because it is possible for us to do otherwise.[16]

No matter what kind of evil we face, we are not powerless. Through God we are designed to act. Through Jesus we are freed from the sin that keeps us from acting. Through the Holy Spirit we have the power to act. Let's act! The missionaries of the future won't just be translating Bibles and teaching classes. They'll be healing bodies, leading peace negotiations, building structures and systems that protect people from natural disasters, fighting tyranny, championing economic growth, battling pollution and disease, prosecuting crime, and spreading technology and education—all in Jesus's name.

In the light of the cross, we can see clearly what is right and wrong, good and evil. And because of the cross, we have hope that God will conquer evil. In fact, the entire story of the Bible is how he is doing just that.

What Must We Do Now?

I love New Year's Eve, but not just for the celebrations. In my Bible-reading plan, December 31 covers the last three chapters of Revelation. This is a favorite verse: "He will wipe away every tear from their eyes, and death shall be no more, neither shall there be mourning, nor crying, nor pain anymore, for the former things have passed away" (21:4). In the final chapters of the Bible's last book, I'm reminded that a redeemed world is a greater testament to God's glory than creation itself.

On January 1, I read the first three chapters of Genesis, which tell about the creation of the world and of man and woman and about humanity's fall. Deceit and sin are depressing, but because of the previous day's reading in Revelation, I study the beginning with the end in mind.

In the garden, death came to those who disobeyed God. In God's future city, there is no more death or sorrow. At the end of all things, Satan, the deceiver, loses all further influence. The pain that multiplied in the garden vanishes when God comes to make his home among his people. The sin that broke Adam's dominion is overcome by Jesus.

The first paradise is closed, but the second paradise will be open for business. No longer will we be driven from God's presence; indeed, we shall see his face (Rev. 22:4).

From Genesis to Revelation the Bible presents us with a vibrant God. It makes today's misguided view of God as a kindly old man who wants us to be happy seem shriveled. God isn't merely a grandfather who lets us have as many ice-cream bars as we want. He is the rescuing king who's redeeming what he has made. Through Jesus he is making all things new (Rev. 21:5).

So, instead of settling for pithy pronouncements such as "God is good all the time," I've decided to change tactics.

Ask questions. The goal of questions is to draw people closer to God and leave them in thought. When someone says, "I could never believe in a God who would allow evil," I ask, "Would you tell me your story? How did you arrive at that conclusion?" When someone tells me something ought not to be, I ask, "Can you tell me how you know what ought to be? Is that just your preference, or is it based on something true? Where did that truth come from?" If someone rejects a biblical explanation of good and evil, I ask, "What does your worldview say about where evil comes from and how to restore what is good?"

Move in close. Years before Stephanie and I married, I found myself sinking into depression over my divorce and the pressures of being a single dad. During that time, I took a break from the office and drove to an overlook in Garden of the Gods, a park containing majestic rock formations in Colorado Springs. Ordinarily it's a peaceful spot where I find restoration. This day, though, the beauty of my surroundings seemed to taunt me about the disarray of my life. I wondered, *Do I want to go on?* At that very moment my phone rang. "This is Boomer," said a friendly voice. "Honey and I wanted to see how you're doing." Boomer and Honey—pet names for my kids' adopted grandparents. Having lost a son to suicide, they were drawn to my pain rather than repelled by it. To this day I don't remember what they shared in that call, but it felt as if I were speaking with angels. This wasn't because of their words; it was because of their instinct to move in close.

Share about heaven. Randy Alcorn reminded us that "evil is temporary; God's goodness and our joy will be eternal."[17] We cannot fully comprehend the description of the new creation in the book of Revelation. There will be no sun and no sea, for example, and no sin (21:1, 23, 27). But what we can comprehend is extremely exciting: we won't just be floating around on clouds playing harps. We'll be able to watch God at work—and we'll work alongside him—making all things new.

Most importantly, give the reason for my hope. During the season of darkness following my divorce, I read a book called *Shattered Dreams* by Larry Crabb. On the very first page of the book, he said, "God is not waiting to bless us after our troubles end. He is blessing us right now, in and through those troubles. At this exact moment, He is giving us what He thinks is good."[18] I wrote this quote on an index card and posted it on my bathroom mirror. God is not aloof. He is right here. Jesus has promised, "In the world you will have tribulation. But take heart; I have overcome the world" (John 16:33). Hope has arrived and is rallying the hopeless to God's banner of love.

———

The truth is, my toughest questions may never be answered this side of eternity. As I write this, Stephanie is feeling better. Her stamina is returning. Yet, despite our prayers, the blood clot that caused Stephanie's rare stroke hasn't reduced in size. "It might never go away," one specialist conceded.

"It's like I have a time bomb in my head," Stephanie has truthfully reflected. When you think about it, we're all in a similar predicament. No person on this planet is more than one heartbeat away from eternity.

With this uncertainty, Stephanie and I have decided to treat every day as a gift. We don't know how many days God will give her. Or me, for that matter. But treating each day as a gift has changed the way we think about God, other people, and, well, everything.

God is indeed good all the time, but not because *I* like what he is doing for *me* right now. God's goodness is not an argument or a pronouncement. It's a person—Jesus. At the cross, God declared victory. As the apostle Paul wrote in 1 Corinthians 15:55, "O death, where is your victory? O death, where is your sting?"

Through Christ, meaning emerges out of emptiness. *In* Christ, healing rises out of pain. *Because of* Christ, God not only makes good possible but also makes good happen. When I think about it, this is a truth that ties together all of the unquestioned answers we've talked about. The only question I have left is "What's next?"

Discussion Questions

1. What are your first thoughts when you hear "God is good"?

2. What are some times in your life when you have struggled to believe that God is good?

3. Where do you see evidence of God's goodness in your life?

4. How can we share God's goodness with others while acknowledging the reality of pain and evil in our fallen world?

Conclusion

Out of the Shallows, into the Deep

"Big step now," said the weathered Florida boat captain cheerily.

Pressing the scuba mask and regulator to my face, I put one huge fin forward into space and let gravity do its thing. Down I went, splashing through the water's surface and back up again like a cork.

Glancing around, I realized I was much farther from the boat than I had expected to be. *The captain wasn't kidding about the strong current,* I thought.

A few yards away, the dive guide noticed my concerned look and called out, gesturing, "Swim over here and grab this line."

Finning my way in her direction, I reached up and grasped the nylon rope stretching from the boat to a nearby descent line. I could see the other divers, including my two teenage children, bobbing in the rough water. Suddenly a wave slapped me in the face and dislodged my air source.

Choking and spitting, I glanced sheepishly at the guide. Rookie mistake. She smiled and said, "You're good. Just put your snorkel in to save air until the descent. And then *look down*."

I did as she instructed. Although I had accumulated nearly fifty dives, nothing prepared me for what I saw spread out on the ocean floor ninety feet below.

———

Scuba diving is one of my hobbies when I have the money and time, which is about once every year or two. Adding to the expense is the anxiety. Every time I step off a perfectly good boat into a seemingly endless ocean, my heart pounds with uncertainty.

The payoff, though, is huge. God hid some of his most fascinating creations beneath the waves, including the parrotfish, goliath grouper, moray eel, spider crab, and blue-ringed octopus. Within the vast oceans are millions of animal and plant species that few people will ever see in their natural habitats.

That day off the Florida coast, I stuffed the snorkel in my mouth and looked down. In the murky depths I could make out the superstructure of an enormous sunken ship. For years my kids and I had worked, saved, and trained for this day—our first wreck dive.

I wondered how many people had traveled over this exact spot, oblivious to the historical treasure resting silently in the depths below. Then, as I stared, my gaze fell on a dozen barracuda patiently waiting near the descent line. Oh great. What's below the surface is cool but also sometimes a little … complicated. Fortunately for the divers, the barracuda were there for the fish, not for us.

In the world of ideas, like in the ocean, many people settle for surface-level answers to life's deepest questions. Doing so seems sensible. It satisfactorily settles most issues and prevents bickering. Unfortunately, prepackaged solutions only float on the surface. They keep us in the shallows when breathtaking wonder awaits those willing to go a little deeper.

As you'll recall from the beginning of the book, *Unquestioned Answers* is a call to reject Simplicism. The antidote to unquestioned answers is sometimes better answers. Other times it's better questions. With that in mind, we dove below the surface of ten simplistic slogans to find unwavering biblical truths about God, the world, and the people we interact with every day.

Let's review the clichés we examined on our brief journey and the conclusions that emerged.

1. *"God said it; I believe it; that settles it for me."* Alone among history's influential religious books, the Bible calls for the reader to examine its truth. The Bible records many mysteries, but it does not shroud in secrecy the most important revelation in all the world: there is a God who speaks to everyone everywhere about everything. It's a book for all his people. God welcomes our inquiries.

2. *"Just have faith."* We all place faith in something. The question is whether the object of our faith is worthy. Biblically, faith does not mean believing things that don't match up to reality. It means admitting that God *is* the greatest reality in the universe, who solves the mysteries of knowledge and existence, bringing healing

and purpose to our lives. Faith in God isn't something we *have*; it's something we *live*.

3. *"God will heal our land if we humble ourselves and pray."* We don't need to twist God's hands behind his back by holding him to a promise that was not made to us. The testimony of Scripture, especially through the words of Jesus, shows us that the almighty Sovereign of the universe has invited us to ask and promised to answer. That's a lot better than any prayer formula.

4. *"It's just me and Jesus."* The "me-ness" of "me and Jesus" is precisely what I need to be rescued from. To find redemption, I must first admit I can't save myself. The path to purpose is outside myself. The biggest dreams are given to characters whose stories are larger than they can tell by themselves. This larger story is the story of the church. Being in community with other believers is the only way we become mature spiritually.

5. *"Love the sinner; hate the sin."* When we see others as God sees them, we view everything in the light of our own fallenness and Jesus's unimaginable offer of grace. This cliché suggests that others' sins are worse for them than ours are for us. By asking questions and knowing others, we can share Jesus's love and offer of reconciliation with them.

6. *"Christianity is a relationship, not a religion."* If we trust what the Bible says, neither the word *relationship* nor the word *religion* sufficiently portrays the awesome work of God in sending Jesus. He is fully God, the one through whom we can be reconciled to God. A personal relationship with Jesus culminates in robust insight into the cause, nature, and purpose of the universe. That's religion. But this is no dead religion; in relationship with Jesus we can see the

whole world from his viewpoint and proclaim the hope and healing he offers.

7. *"Jesus was a social justice warrior."* Jesus came as the Son of God to reconcile us to God, not to affirm anyone's utopian agenda. At the same time, the salvation we have received ought to restore our capacity to love our neighbors. Because Jesus is the way, the truth, and the life (John 14:6), we can know what justice is, see the truth, and live lives of wholeness and completeness with those around us.

8. *"It's not my place to judge."* Uttering this slogan cuts vital conversations short just when they're becoming meaningful. Instead, we ought to ask questions that display curiosity and friendly determination. Asking, not telling, helps people see past our faults—and their own—through the lens of the Bible's message of restoration.

9. *"This world has nothing for me."* In Christ all things are being made new. Relationships violently ruptured in the fall can be restored. Walls can be repaired. The path to God and eternal purpose can be cleared of brush and followed once again. The Bible says that God has called creation "very good" (Gen. 1:31) and made it clear that we are to spread shalom until he tells us to stop. We can experience peace with God and proclaim it to the generations after us.

10. *"God is good all the time—all the time God is good."* God is indeed good all the time, not just when *I* like what he is doing for *me* right now. God's answer to evil is a person—Jesus. At the cross God declared victory. Our toughest questions may never be answered this side of eternity, but each day is a gift God has given us to bring glory to him and do good to our neighbors.

If you remember nothing else about these ten clichés, remember this: the most questionable thing about unquestioned answers is how they put the focus on me—what I like, what I'm comfortable with, and what makes sense to me.

Life isn't about me. Nor would I want it to be. Imagine that I settled into my seat in Los Angeles's El Capitan Theatre for a much-anticipated movie screening only to discover that the featured presentation consisted of two hours of my random smartphone videos stitched together. I would probably be the only one to remain in the theater, and I doubt even I'd stay the whole time.

When I go to the movies, I want to be changed. When the lights go down and the screen flickers to life, I want to be transported to another world where the characters are transformed. I want their experiences to transform me too. Good art and music displace us from the center of our own worlds. Watching an epic sporting event such as the Olympics does this. So does watching the sunset. Extraordinary performances impart grace and courage to live our days differently from that moment forward.

This same kind of transformation becomes possible when we leave behind simplistic clichés and seek biblical truth. Rethinking leads to rediscovery, which leads to renewal.

Spiritual transformation is not merely about sharpening our words or learning to chant along with our tribe. Instead, the Bible's story moves God to the center of the world's story—and of our own. There's a challenge here. God's truth doesn't feather my nest; it pushes me out of it.

The world the Bible describes isn't a stick drawing or a paint-by-numbers picture. It's a teeming, chirping burst of color and texture over which falls a menacing shadow, until the darkness is complete and God's Son dies of his wounds and the earth shakes and the temple veil is torn in two.

But then history pivots in a new direction. Jesus conquers death, sweeping aside the veil covering our hearts and minds. He is alive, and we may behold his glory and be transformed (2 Cor. 3:18).

This is not a onetime transformation. It's ongoing change taking place every day of our lives. I found this to be especially true during a painful season of depression. With each new sunrise, I groaned, *God, I just can't do another year like this*. Then Scripture would flood my mind about God's mercies being new every morning (Lam. 3:22–23). *Let's not do another year*, God seemed to be saying. *Let's do today*. Every day offers an opportunity to reject Simplicism and go deep so we can grow.

On a recent scuba diving trip, as I reflected on God's glory in creation, I found myself obsessed with checking and rechecking the tank, hoses, and regulator, without which I would instantly suffocate. Oddly, as this happened, my mind rewound to the story that opened this book: my suffocating experience as a fourth grader at a private Christian school. It took years to realize that it wasn't small-minded faith that was suffocating me; it was my own reluctance to yield my will to Jesus. God isn't shaping me into the image of my pastor or the athlete who always gives a shout-out to God or the impressive business leader who credits faith for her success. He's shaping me into the image of his Son in a process that is nothing like the clicking, shuffling din of an assembly line. Rather, it's a work of art that takes a lifetime to complete.

The Bible points us true. Consider *Unquestioned Answers* to be your logbook recording your first ten dives. Look at all the pages still left to write—all the adventures still to be had! Down we go, beyond the small talk to the quiet place where fish pirouette among the swaying coral, moving to an inaudible symphony. Down, down to the place where we can know God—that he is worthy of faith, that he has called us to great deeds, and that, above all, he is good.

Discussion Questions

1. What are some clichés you're going to think differently about now?

2. Are there any clichés you disagree with me about? Why? Why not?

3. What are some practical steps you would like to take to counteract Simplicism?

Notes

Introduction

1. Aaron Earls, "Most Teenagers Drop Out of Church as Young Adults," LifeWay Research, January 15, 2019, https://lifewayresearch.com/2019/01/15/most -teenagers-drop-out-of-church-as-young-adults.

2. Caitlin Johnson, "Cutting through Advertising Clutter," *CBS News,* September 17, 2006, www.cbsnews.com/8301-3445_162-2015684.html.

3. "Religion among the Millennials," Pew Research Center, February 17, 2010, www.pewforum.org/2010/02/17/religion-among-the-millennials.

4. A helpful article about what happens in the brain when we think hard and reflect deeply is Jeffrey Kluger et al., "Is God in Our Genes?," *Time,* October 25, 2004. A popular author on the subject is Carolyn Leaf. See, for example, *Think, Learn, Succeed: Understanding and Using Your Mind to Thrive at School, the Workplace, and Life* (Grand Rapids, MI: Baker, 2018).

5. Alex Harris and Brett Harris, "Noah Riner: Faith under Fire at Dartmouth," accessed August 16, 2019, www.therebelution.com/blog/2005/10/noah-riner -faith-under-fire-at-dartmouth; Erin Curry, "Culture Digest: Dartmouth Student Lambasted for Esteeming Jesus in Convocation Speech; Victoria's

Secret Displays Draw Ire," *Baptist Press*, October 12, 2005, www.bpnews.net
/21838/culture-digest-dartmouth-student-lambasted-for-esteeming-jesus-in
-convocation-speech-victorias-secret-displays-draw-ire.

Chapter 1

1. David Wilkerson, "Doubt—the Sin That God Hates Most," World Challenge,
April 2, 2001, https://worldchallenge.org/newsletter/doubt-%E2%80%94
-sin-god-hates-most.

2. Charles Haddon Spurgeon, "The Lover of God's Law Filled with Peace" (sermon,
Metropolitan Tabernacle, London, January 22, 1888), www.spurgeon.org
/resource-library/sermons/the-lover-of-gods-law-filled-with-peace#flipbook.

3. Heritage Singers, "God Said It, I Believe It," 1976, video, 3:33, September 27,
2009, www.youtube.com/watch?v=924MCB12MfA.

4. Jonathan Morrow, *Welcome to College: A Christ-Follower's Guide for the Journey*
(Grand Rapids, MI: Kregel, 2008), 88.

5. James B. Green, quoted in John F. Walvoord, *The Holy Spirit: A Comprehensive
Study of the Person and Work of the Holy Spirit* (Grand Rapids, MI: Zondervan,
1991), 61.

6. See David S. Dockery, *Christian Scripture: An Evangelical Perspective on
Inspiration, Authority, and Interpretation* (Eugene, OR: Wipf and Stock, 2004),
64; Douglas Groothuis, *Christian Apologetics: A Comprehensive Case for Biblical
Faith* (Downers Grove, IL: InterVarsity, 2011); John R. W. Stott, *The Authority
of the Bible* (Downers Grove, IL: InterVarsity, 1974).

7. Kevin DeYoung put it this way: "Our Messiah sees himself as an expositor of
Scripture, but never a corrector of Scripture. He fulfills it, but never falsifies it.
He turns away wrong interpretations of Scripture, but insists there is nothing
wrong with Scripture, down to the crossing of t's and dotting of i's." *Taking
God at His Word: Why the Bible Is Knowable, Necessary, and Enough, and What
That Means for You and Me* (Wheaton, IL: Crossway, 2014), 102.

8. See, for example, Matthew 7:28–29 and Mark 2:8–12.

9. Specifically Jesus claimed authority over the Sabbath (Mark 2:27–28), to forgive
sin (v. 5), to perform miracles (vv. 8–9), to raise himself from the dead (John
2:19–22), over the angels (Matt. 13:41), over the kingdom of God (v. 41),

over the prophets throughout the centuries (23:34), and over judgment of all the world (25:31–46; 26:63–65; John 5:22, 27).

10. Garry K. Brantley, "The Dead Sea Scrolls and Biblical Integrity," Apologetics Press, accessed August 17, 2019, www.apologeticspress.org/apcontent .aspx?category=13&article=357; The Leon Levy Dead See Scrolls Digital Library, Israel Antiquities Authority, accessed September 16, 2019, www.deadseascrolls.org.il/learn-about-the-scrolls/discovery-sites?locale=en_US.

11. Philip R. Davies, *In Search of "Ancient Israel"* (1992; repr., London: Continuum, 2006), 12.

12. Israel Finkelstein, quoted in Jeffery L. Sheler, *Is the Bible True? How Modern Debates and Discoveries Affirm the Essence of Scripture* (New York: HarperCollins, 2000), 96.

13. Lazar Berman, "Archaeologists Say They've Found One of King David's Palaces," *Times of Israel*, July 18, 2013, www.timesofisrael.com/archaeologists-say-one -of-king-davids-palaces-found.

14. Sheler, *Is the Bible True?*, 254. If you'd like to read more, I recommend K. A. Kitchen, *On the Reliability of the Old Testament* (Grand Rapids, MI: Eerdmans, 2003). Kitchen is professor emeritus of Egyptology and honorary senior fellow at the Department of Archaeology, Classics, and Egyptology, University of Liverpool, England.

15. Edwin M. Yamauchi, "Jesus outside the New Testament: What Is the Evidence?," in Michael J. Wilkins and J. P. Moreland, eds., *Jesus under Fire: Modern Scholarship Reinvents the Historical Jesus* (Grand Rapids, MI: Zondervan, 1995), 221.

16. An excellent source about the accuracy of the Bible is Josh McDowell and Sean McDowell, *Evidence That Demands a Verdict: Life-Changing Truth for a Skeptical World*, rev. ed. (Nashville: Thomas Nelson, 2017).

17. For more detailed information, see Paul W. Rood II, "The Untold Story of the Fundamentals," *Biola Magazine*, accessed August 23, 2019, http://magazine .biola.edu/article/14-summer/the-untold-story-of-the-fundamentals. A. C. Dixon and R. A. Torrey were two of the editors of the series, which included contributions from James Orr (the Free Church of Scotland's Glasgow college—now Trinity College, Glasgow), B. B. Warfield (Princeton Theological Seminary), and C. I. Scofield (former alcoholic and scandal-plagued attorney turned cofounder of Philadelphia School of the Bible—now Cairn University).

18. Readers interested in the history of evangelicalism might enjoy reading Joel A. Carpenter, *Revive Us Again: The Reawakening of American Fundamentalism* (Oxford: Oxford University Press, 1997); Marvin Olasky and John Perry, *Monkey Business: The True Story of the Scopes Trial* (Nashville: Broadman & Holman, 2005); Richard J. Mouw, *The Smell of Sawdust: What Evangelicals Can Learn from Their Fundamentalist Heritage* (Grand Rapids, MI: Zondervan, 2000); and James Davison Hunter, *Evangelicalism: The Coming Generation* (Chicago: University of Chicago Press, 1987).

19. "Who We Are," World Evangelical Alliance, accessed August 17, 2019, www.worldea.org/whoweare/introduction.

20. Jason Mandryk, referenced in Jennifer Riley, "Mission Expert: Evangelicalism Fastest Growing Religious Movement," *Christian Post*, September 28, 2006, www.christianpost.com/news/mission-expert -evangelicalism-fastest-growing-religious-movement.html.

21. See Alvin J. Schmidt, *How Christianity Changed the World* (Grand Rapids, MI: Zondervan, 2004).

22. Charles Haddon Spurgeon, "Holding Fast the Faith" (sermon, Metropolitan Tabernacle, London, February 5, 1888), www.spurgeon.org/resource-library /sermons/holding-fast-the-faith#flipbook.

Chapter 2

1. Nina Keegan, "Faith Starts Where Logic Fails," CBN, accessed August 17, 2019, www1.cbn.com/Devotions/faith-starts-where-logic-fails.

2. Mark Twain, *Following the Equator: A Journey around the World* (Hartford, CT: American, 1897), 132.

3. Steven Pinker, "Less Faith, More Reason," *Harvard Crimson*, October 27, 2006, www.thecrimson.com/article/2006/10/27/less-faith-more-reason -there-is.

4. Richard Dawkins, quoted in Keith Mathison, "Faith and Reason," Ligonier Ministries, June 1, 2013, www.ligonier.org/learn/articles/faith-and-reason -article.

5. The Greek statement in Mark 11:22 is Ἔχετε πίστιν θεοῦ, literally "Have faith from God," though it is usually translated "Have faith in God."

6. J. P. Moreland, *Love Your God with All Your Mind: The Role of Reason in the Life of the Soul*, rev. ed. (Colorado Springs: NavPress, 2012), 56–57.

7. Timothy Keller, *The Reason for God: Belief in an Age of Skepticism* (New York: Penguin Books, 2018), xxiii.

8. *The Epistle of Mathetes to Diognetus*, trans. James Donaldson and Alexander Roberts, Early Christian Writings, accessed August 23, 2019, www.earlychristianwritings.com/text/diognetus-roberts.html.

9. Josh McDowell and Sean McDowell, *The Unshakable Truth: How You Can Experience the 12 Essentials of a Relevant Faith* (Eugene, OR: Harvest House, 2010), 41; Alan Hirsch, referenced in McDowell and McDowell, *Unshakable Truth*, 31–32.

10. Glenn Sunshine, "Columbanus (540–615)," BreakPoint, October 7, 2011, www.breakpoint.org/2011/10/columbanus-540-615.

11. Glenn Sunshine, "Robert Grosseteste (c. 1170–1253)," BreakPoint, March 25, 2012, www.breakpoint.org/2012/03/robert-grosseteste-c-1170-1253.

12. Glenn Sunshine, "Roger Bacon (c. 1214–1294)," BreakPoint, May 28, 2012, www.breakpoint.org/2012/05/roger-bacon-c-1214-1294.

13. "Amazing Grace," Hymnal.net, accessed September 16, 2019, www.hymnal.net /en/hymn/h/313.

Chapter 3

1. Chris Taylor, "70% of Rich Families Lose Their Wealth by the Second Generation," *Money*, June 17, 2015, http://money.com/money/3925308 /rich-families-lose-wealth.

2. Max Lucado, "The Power of Election Prayer," Max Lucado, accessed August 23, 2019, https://maxlucado.com/the-power-of-election-prayer.

3. Billy Graham (speech, Lincoln Memorial, Washington, DC, July 4, 1970), https://billygraham.org/video/billy-graham-honoring-america.

4. Greg Laurie, "Greg Laurie: 'If You Want to See Revival, Do Revival-Like Things,'" CBN News, September 16, 2018, www1.cbn.com/cbnnews/us/2018 /september/greg-laurie-if-you-want-to-see-revival-do-revival-like-things.

5. H. Richard Niebuhr, *Christ and Culture* (1951; repr., New York: HarperCollins, 2001), 83–92.

6. See Deuteronomy 17:6 and 19:15; see also the apostle Paul's use in 2 Corinthians 13:1 and 1 Timothy 5:19; the author of Hebrews also used the phrase in Hebrews 10:28.

7. The first skill is *hermeneutics* (from the Greek word *hermēneuein*, meaning "to interpret"). Hermeneutics is the large-scale process of devising correct methods of interpreting Scripture. The second skill is *exegesis*, which is the difficult but rewarding small-scale work of wrestling with each chapter, verse, line, and word. Wayne Grudem, *Systematic Theology: An Introduction to Biblical Doctrine* (Grand Rapids, MI: Zondervan, 1994), 108–9.

8. Michael W. Goheen, "Reading the Bible as One Story," accessed August 24, 2019, https://thedramaofscripture.files.wordpress.com/2011/02/reading-the -bible-as-one-story.pdf.

9. A recent anthology of essays from leading experts called *Rethinking Secularism* shows that many people, even highly trained academics, are rethinking the validity of the assumption that God is irrelevant to what's important in life. Craig Calhoun, Mark Juergensmeyer, and Jonathan VanAntwerpen, eds., *Rethinking Secularism* (New York: Oxford University Press, 2011).

10. Jesse Duplantis, quoted in Samuel Osborne, "'It's What Jesus Would Do': Televangelist Asks Followers for $54m to Buy Private Jet," *Independent*, May 29, 2018, www.independent.co.uk/news/world/americas/televangelist-jet-jesse -duplantis-falcon-7x-louisiana-kenneth-copeland-a8374316.html.

11. "Goal 1: End Poverty in All Its Forms Everywhere," United Nations, accessed August 24, 2019, www.un.org/sustainabledevelopment/poverty.

12. Craig Hazen, *Fearless Prayer: Why We Don't Ask and Why We Should* (Eugene, OR: Harvest, 2018), 115.

Chapter 4

1. Brad Paisley, vocalist, "Me and Jesus," by Tom T. Hall, Grand Ole Opry, Nashville, TN, May 2, 2013.

2. Jeremy Weber, "Pew: Why Americans Go to Church or Stay Home," *Christianity Today*, August 1, 2018, www.christianitytoday.com/news/2018 /july/church-attendance-top-reasons-go-or-stay-home-pew.html.

3. Roxanne Stone, quoted in "Meet Those Who 'Love Jesus but Not the Church,'" Barna, March 30, 2017, www.barna.com/research/meet-love-jesus-not-church.

4. Frank Newport, "Five Key Findings on Religion in the U.S.," Gallup, December 23, 2016, https://news.gallup.com/poll/200186/five-key -findings-religion.aspx?g_source=link_newsv9&g_campaign=item _232226&g_medium=copy.

5. Regular church attendance is defined as at least twice a month. Aaron Earls, "Most Teenagers Drop Out of Church as Young Adults," LifeWay Research, January 15, 2019, https://lifewayresearch.com/2019/01/15/most-teenagers -drop-out-of-church-as-young-adults.

6. Mark D. Regnerus and Jeremy E. Uecker, "How Corrosive Is College to Religious Faith and Practice?," Social Science Research Council, February 5, 2007, http://religion.ssrc.org/reforum/Regnerus_Uecker.pdf.

7. "What Is Sticky Faith?," Fuller Youth Institute, accessed August 24, 2019, https://fulleryouthinstitute.org/stickyfaith.

8. For a broader overview of the personal and social value of religious communities, see Dennis Prager, *The Rational Bible: Genesis—God, Creation, and Destruction* (Washington, DC: Regnery Faith, 2019), especially the discussion of Genesis 2:18.

9. Matt Redman, *The Unquenchable Worshipper: Coming Back to the Heart of Worship* (Ventura, CA: Regal, 2001), 18.

10. Alexander Schmemann, *For the Life of the World: Sacraments and Orthodoxy* (Crestwood, NY: St. Vladimir's Seminary Press, 2004), 26.

11. Parker J. Palmer, *Let Your Life Speak: Listening for the Voice of Vocation* (San Francisco: Jossey-Bass, 2000), 108.

12. Ralph Mattson and Arthur Miller, *Finding a Job You Can Love* (Nashville: Thomas Nelson, 1982), 172.

13. Mattson and Miller, *Finding a Job You Can Love*, 161.

14. William Damon, *The Path to Purpose: How Young People Find Their Calling in Life* (New York: Free Press, 2008), xi–xii, 10.

15. David B. Feldman, "Is Religion Good or Bad for Us?," *Psychology Today*, September 10, 2018, www.psychologytoday.com/us/blog/supersurvivors /201809/is-religion-good-or-bad-us.

16. David Kinnaman and Gabe Lyons, *unChristian: What a New Generation Really Thinks about Christianity … and Why It Matters* (Grand Rapids, MI: Baker, 2007), 28, 48.

17. "5 Reasons Millennials Stay Connected to Church," Barna, September 17, 2013, www.barna.org/barna-update/millennials/635-5-reasons-millennials -stay-connected-to-church.

18. This is one of many conclusions reached by Jason Lanker in "The Relationship between Mid-Adolescent Natural Mentoring and the Christian Spirituality of North American First-Year Christian College Students" (PhD diss., Talbot School of Theology, Biola University, 2009), 141, 147.

19. To explore this topic further, you might start with a book and curriculum I've written for churches called *Grow Together*, www.summit.org/books-media /grow-together-small-group-study. See also Monika Ardelt, "Effects of Religion and Purpose in Life on Elders' Subjective Well Being and Attitudes toward Death," *Journal of Religious Gerontology* 14, no. 4 (2003): 55–77. Ardelt reported that activities that increase a person's sense of well-being may have a profound effect on fundamental aspects of his or her psychology. In turn, a high level of purpose in life was associated with a reduced risk of mortality among older persons. When it comes to the power of mentoring, there are many studies demonstrating these effects. See, for example, Andrew J. Martin and Martin Dowson, "Interpersonal Relationships, Motivation, Engagement, and Achievement: Yields for Theory, Current Issues, and Educational Practice," *Review of Educational Research* 79, no. 1 (2009): 344; Kathryn R. Wentzel, "Social-Motivational Processes and Interpersonal Relationships: Implications for Understanding Motivation at School," *Journal of Educational Psychology* 91, no. 1 (1999): 76–97; Andrew J. Martin et al., "Getting Along with Teachers and Parents: The Yields of Good Relationships for Students' Achievement Motivation and Self-Esteem," *Australian Journal of Guidance and Counselling* 17, no. 2 (2007): 109–25; Barbara Fresko and Cheruta Wertheim, "Learning by Mentoring: Prospective Teachers as Mentors to Children at-Risk," *Mentoring and Tutoring* 14, no. 2 (2006): 149–61; and Keith A. King et al., "Increasing Self-Esteem and School Connectedness through a Multidimensional Mentoring Program," *Journal of School Health* 72, no. 7 (2002): 294–99.

Chapter 5

1. Lauren Daigle, quoted in Jonathan Merritt, "Lauren Daigle and the Lost Art of Discernment," *Atlantic*, December 8, 2018, www.theatlantic.com/ideas/archive /2018/12/let-lauren-daigle-be-unsure-about-lgbt-relationships/577651.

2. Kim Burrell, quoted in Maeve McDermott, "Singer Kim Burrell Booted from 'Ellen' after Calling Gay People 'Perverted,'" *USA Today*, January 3, 2017, www.usatoday.com/story/life/2017/01/03/singer-kim-burrell-booted-ellen -after-calling-gay-people-perverted/96119370.

3. Christopher Yuan, *Holy Sexuality and the Gospel: Sex, Desire, and Relationships Shaped by God's Grand Story* (Colorado Springs: Multnomah, 2018), 168–69.

4. Yuan, *Holy Sexuality*, 168.

5. Jonathan Merritt, "One Problem with Kim Burrell's 'Hate the Sin, Love the Sinner' Argument," *USA Today*, January 4, 2017, www.usatoday.com/story /news/2017/01/04/kim-burrell-hate-the-sin-love-the-sinner/96158416.

6. Augustine, "Letter 211," in *The Works of Saint Augustine: A Translation for the 21st Century, part 2, Letters*, vol. 4, *Letters 211–270, 1*–29**, ed. Boniface Ramsey, trans. Roland Teske (Hyde Park, NY: New City, 2005), 19.

7. The evidence that humans have a special place in creation includes the following: (1) humans were created last—all creation seemed to be preparation for humanity's arrival; (2) humans were the product of divine deliberation—God said "Let us make man in our image" (Gen. 1:26); (3) the description of the creation of humans is more intensive and extensive than any other creative act; (4) Scripture uses the special word for "create" (*bara'*), which always involves a special creative act of God (1:1, 21, 27; 2:3); (5) while other acts of creation were described as "good," the completion of creation and the creation of humanity were evaluated by God as "very good" (1:31); and (6) as bearers of God's image, humanity possesses an exalted status over other creatures (v. 26).

8. "Strong's H8104—*Shamar*," Blue Letter Bible, accessed August 25, 2019, www.blueletterbible.org/lang/lexicon/lexicon.cfm?Strongs=H8104&t=KJV; Richard T. Ritenbaugh, quoted in "Bible Verses about Shamar," Bible Tools, accessed August 25, 2019, www.bibletools.org/index.cfm/fuseaction/Topical .show/RTD/cgg/ID/2169/Shamar.htm.

9. Niall McCarthy, "Report: Americans More Likely to Die from Opioid Overdoses Than Car Crashes," *Forbes*, January 15, 2019, www.forbes.com /sites/microsoft365/2019/07/18/behind-the-shift/#46a7eb545313.

10. Amanda MacMillan, "Mental Illness Is on the Rise in the U.S. for a Frustrating Reason," *Health*, April 18, 2017, www.health.com/depression /8-million-americans-psychological-distress.

11. Maggie Fox, "Major Depression on the Rise among Everyone, New Data Shows," NBC News, May 10, 2018, www.nbcnews.com/health/health-news /major-depression-rise-among-everyone-new-data-shows-n873146; "Suicide by Age," Suicide Prevention Resource Center, accessed August 25, 2019, www.sprc.org/scope/age.

12. Holly Ellyatt, "US Is Seeing 'Relentless Rise in Household Wealth,' Credit Suisse Report Says," CNBC, October 18, 2018, www.cnbc.com/2018/10/18/credit -suisse-wealth-report-show-relentless-rise-in-household-wealth.html; Steve Hargreaves, "15% of Americans Living in Poverty," CNN, September 17, 2013, https://money.cnn.com/2013/09/17/news/economy/poverty-income.

13. "Children Make Up Almost One-Third of All Human Trafficking Victims Worldwide," UNICEF, July 27, 2018, www.unicef.org/stories/children -make-almost-one-third-all-human-trafficking-victims-worldwide.

14. See Albert M. Wolters, *Creation Regained: Biblical Basics for a Reformational Worldview* (Grand Rapids, MI: Eerdmans, 2005), 46.

15. Wolters, *Creation Regained*, 46.

16. Timothy Keller, *Counterfeit Gods: The Empty Promises of Money, Sex, and Power, and the Only Hope That Matters* (New York: Riverhead Books, 2011), 172.

17. Yuan, *Holy Sexuality*, 167–68.

18. Yuan, *Holy Sexuality*, 170.

19. Charles Colson, *Against the Night: Living in the New Dark Ages* (Ann Arbor, MI: Vine Books, 1999), 151–52.

Chapter 6

1. Quoted in Amos Elon, "The Excommunication of Hannah Arendt," *World Policy Journal* 23, no. 4 (Winter 2007): 97.

2. Maximilian Kolbe, quoted in Alyssa Murphy, "St. Maximilian Kolbe's Martyrdom Tells True Story of Sacrifice," *National Catholic Register*, August 14, 2019, www.ncregister.com/blog/alyssamurphy/rare-photos-released-of-st .-maximilian-kolbe-tell-true-story-of-sacrifice.

3. Franciszek Gajowniczek, quoted in Zita Ballinger Fletcher, "German Church Hosts Maximilian Kolbe Mass at Auschwitz," *National Catholic Reporter*,

accessed August 26, 2019, www.ncronline.org/news/people/german-church
-hosts-maximilian-kolbe-mass-auschwitz.

4. George Weigel, *Witness to Hope: The Biography of Pope John Paul II* (New York: Harper Perennial, 2005), 78, 447.

5. Filip Mazurczak, "How Saint John Paul II Conquered Communism," *Catholic World Report*, June 16, 2016, www.catholicworldreport.com/2016/06/16/how -saint-john-paul-ii-conquered-communism.

6. Palash Ghosh, "How Many People Did Joseph Stalin Kill?," *International Business Times*, March 5, 2013, www.ibtimes.com/how-many-people-did -joseph-stalin-kill-1111789.

7. Joel Kotkin, "Why Social Justice Is Killing Synagogues and Churches," *Tablet*, March 1, 2019, www.tabletmag.com/jewish-news-and-politics/281276/social -justice-is-killing-synagogues.

8. Carol Pipes, "SBC Leaders Lament Lack of Evangelistic Passion Evidenced by Annual Report," LifeWay Newsroom, May 28, 2014, https://blog.lifeway.com /newsroom/2014/05/28/sbc-leaders-lament-lack-of-evangelistic-passion -evidenced-by-annual-report/.

9. *"Belief in God,"* Religious Landscape Study, Pew Research Center, www.pewforum.org/religious-landscape-study/belief-in-god; Michael Lipka and Claire Gecewicz, "More Americans Now Say They're Spiritual but Not Religious," Pew Research Center, September 6, 2017, www.pewresearch.org /fact-tank/2017/09/06/more-americans-now-say-theyre-spiritual-but-not -religious.

10. Jefferson Bethke, "Why I Hate Religion, but Love Jesus: Spoken Word," video, 4:03, January 10, 2012, www.youtube.com/watch?v=1IAhDGYlpqY.

11. C. S. Lewis, *Mere Christianity* (New York: HarperOne, 2001), 74.

12. J. Warner Wallace, a highly regarded homicide detective, demonstrated in his book *Cold-Case Christianity* how detectives discern the truth from the clues they find. He applied these techniques to understanding and appreciating the truth of the Gospels. J. Warner Wallace, *Cold-Case Christianity: A Homicide Detective Investigates the Claims of the Gospels* (Colorado Springs: David C Cook, 2013).

13. *Merriam-Webster*, s.v. "fiat," accessed August 26, 2019, www.merriam-webster .com/dictionary/fiat.

14. For more information, see Francis S. Collins, *The Language of God: A Scientist Presents Evidence for Belief* (New York: Free Press, 2007).

15. Kenneth J. Turner summarized the context of Genesis 1 in chapter 6, "Teaching Genesis 1 at a Christian College," of *Reading Genesis 1–2: An Evangelical Conversation*, ed. J. Daryl Charles (Peabody, MA: Hendrickson, 2013).

16. Rob Bell, in "'The Heretic'—Official Trailer—Rob Bell Documentary," video, 2:56, January 31, 2018, www.youtube.com/watch?v=fQ3HYWFhoKg.

17. Sally Lloyd-Jones, *The Jesus Storybook Bible: Every Story Whispers His Name* (Grand Rapids, MI: Zonderkidz, 2007), 17.

18. Glenn Sunshine, "Chiune Sugihara (1900–1986)," BreakPoint, March 1, 2013, www.breakpoint.org/2013/03/chiune-sugihara-1900-1986.

19. "Sugihara Timeline," PBS, accessed August 26, 2019, www.pbs.org/wgbh /sugihara/timeline/text.html.

Chapter 7

1. Andrew Chung, "Ciudad Juárez, Mexico: The World's Most Dangerous Place?," *Toronto Star*, May 21, 2010, www.thestar.com/news/world/2010/05/21/ciudad _jurez_mexico_the_worlds_most_dangerous_place.html.

2. Mark Lacey and Ginger Thompson, "Two Drug Slayings in Mexico Rock U.S. Consulate," *New York Times*, March 14, 2010, www.nytimes.com/2010/03 /15/world/americas/15juarez.html?mtrref=www.google.com&gwh=8CF4C6 1841519E196BCC376137330B8D&gwt=pay&assetType=REGIWALL.

3. "The Statement on Social Justice and the Gospel," SJ&G, accessed August 27, 2019, https://statementonsocialjustice.com.

4. John Pavlovitz, "Jesus Was a Social Justice Warrior," September 15, 2018, John Pavlovitz, https://johnpavlovitz.com/2018/09/15/the-real-statement-on-social -justice-the-gospel/?fbclid=IwAR3QGTZCMfNY9VuJBBNw7Rqsv7gfadKa6c QFFra7Dre10hpGCLYXo3mMkvY.

5. Christopher J. H. Wright, *Old Testament Ethics for the People of God* (Downers Grove, IL: IVP Academic, 2004), 237.

6. Timothy Keller, *Generous Justice: How God's Grace Makes Us Just* (New York: Riverhead Books, 2012), 14. Keller balanced this claim by pointing his readers toward personal sacrifice, not toward a political ideology. In fact, he said, when social justice becomes government enforced, it loses both its "social" and its "justice" meanings.

7. Lexico, s.v. "social justice," accessed August 27, 2019, www.lexico.com/en /definition/social_justice.

8. See Thomas Sowell, *The Quest for Cosmic Justice* (New York: Free Press, 1999), 8.

9. Karl Marx and Frederick Engels, *Collected Works*, vol. 3, Marx and Engels: 1843–1844 (New York: International, 1975), 463. See also David B. T. Aikman's PhD dissertation titled "The Role of Atheism in the Marxist Tradition" (PhD diss., University of Washington, 1979). Aikman covers all aspects of Marxist atheism in his five-hundred-plus-page dissertation.

10. David O. Beale, *In Pursuit of Purity: American Fundamentalism since 1850* (Greenville, SC: Unusual, 1986), 77.

11. Later, the complexities surrounding the social gospel were compounded when a group of Roman Catholic theologians in Latin America tried to reconcile revolutionary Marxism with the Bible. In 1971 a Peruvian priest named Gustavo Gutiérrez wrote *A Theology of Liberation* to argue that "God speaks primarily through the poor and that the Bible can be understood only when seen from the perspective of the poor." *Encyclopaedia Britannica Online*, s.v. "Liberation theology," accessed August 27, 2019, www.britannica.com/topic /liberation-theology.

12. See Jonathan Burnside, *God, Justice, and Society: Aspects of Law and Legality in the Bible* (New York: Oxford University Press, 2011).

13. See www.sledtest.org for how four points—size, level of development, environment, and degree of dependency—form an acronym, *SLED*, which in turn forms an extremely strong argument against elective abortion and other issues relating to bioethics.

14. Lord Atkin (1867–1944) said, "The rule that you are to love your neighbour becomes in law: You must not injure your neighbour, and the lawyer's question: Who is my neighbour? receives a restricted reply. You must take reasonable care to avoid acts or omissions which you can reasonably foresee would be likely to injure your neighbour. Who then, in law, is my neighbour? The answer seems to be persons who are so closely and directly affected by my act that I ought reasonably to have them in contemplation as being so affected when I am directing my mind to the acts or omissions which are called in question." James Richard Atkin, quoted in Carol Harlow, *Understanding Tort Law*, 3rd ed. (London: Sweet & Maxwell, 2005), 47–48.

15. See, for example, Deuteronomy 10:12; Isaiah 40:3; and Jeremiah 6:16. For more academic research, see Joel F. Williams, "Way," in David Noel Freedman, Allen C. Myers, and Astrid B. Beck, eds., *Eerdmans Dictionary of the Bible* (Grand Rapids, MI: Eerdmans, 2000), 1370–71.

16. Aleksandr I. Solzhenitsyn, *The Gulag Archipelago, 1918–1956: An Experiment in Literary Investigation*, trans. Thomas P. Whitney (New York: Harper & Row, 1973), 168.

17. Brian Skaret, "Brian Skaret: Christian Calling and Law Enforcement," interview by John Stonestreet, April 9, 2018, in *BreakPoint Podcast*, podcast, 26:14, www.breakpoint.org/2018/04/brian-skaret-christian-calling-and-law-enforcement.

Chapter 8

1. David Van Biema, "Christianity's Image Problem," *Time*, October 2, 2007, http://content.time.com/time/nation/article/0,8599,1667639,00.html.

2. According to the poll conducted in 2017, 29 percent of churchgoing Christians under forty-five agreed with this statement. Just 8 percent of churchgoing Christians over forty-five agreed. "World Views Study" (unpublished research data), Barna, 27.

3. Eric Wargo, "How Many Seconds to a First Impression?," *Association for Psychological Science*, July 1, 2006, www.psychologicalscience.org/observer /how-many-seconds-to-a-first-impression.

4. Ben Sasse, *Them: Why We Hate Each Other—and How to Heal* (New York: St. Martin's, 2018), 5.

5. Pope Francis, quoted in Joshua J. McElwee, "Francis Explains 'Who Am I to Judge?,'" *National Catholic Reporter*, January 10, 2016, www.ncronline.org /news/vatican/francis-explains-who-am-i-judge.

6. Bob Marley, vocalist, "Judge Not," by Bob Marley, track 1 on *Songs of Freedom*, Island Records, 1992.

7. Garrett J. DeWeese and J. P. Moreland, *Philosophy Made Slightly Less Difficult: A Beginner's Guide to Life's Big Questions* (Downers Grove, IL: IVP Academic, 2005), 56–63.

8. In this list, Richard Beis included prohibition of incest within the nuclear family, prohibition of rape, the demand for some form of marriage, prohibition of adultery (with only a few strictly limited legal exceptions), opposition to promiscuity in the sense of having a large number of partners, the belief that lifelong union of the spouses is the ideal, and exogamy (marriage outside the family) as a further determination of the incest rule.

9. Richard H. Beis, "Some Contributions of Anthropology to Ethics," *Thomist* 27, no. 2 (April 1964): 174–223. Cited in William D. Gairdner, *The Book of Absolutes: A Critique of Relativism and a Defense of Universals* (Montreal: McGill-Queen's University Press, 2008), 198–200.

10. See Anthony Pratkanis and Elliot Aronson, *Age of Propaganda: The Everyday Use and Abuse of Persuasion*, rev. ed. (New York: Henry Holt, 2002), 11. See also Jacques Ellul, *Propaganda: The Formation of Men's Attitudes* (New York: Vintage Books, 1973). Ellul said that propaganda is largely a modern technique made possible by psychological and sociological insights into what moves people. Propaganda makes people feel they are part of a mass movement while, in fact, isolating them from the truth.

11. Ellul, *Propaganda*, 6.

12. Recall the Bible story of Jesus visiting the temple as a twelve-year-old boy. The Bible says that his parents found him asking questions of the religious leaders (Luke 2:46–47). In the Hebrew culture, asking intelligent questions showed that you understood the issues at stake.

13. Elliot Aronson, "The Power of Self-Persuasion," *American Psychologist* 54, no. 11 (November 1999): 875–84.

14. Frank Turek, "Why Would a Good God Allow a Place Like Hell?" (video), Summit Ministries, April 24, 2019, www.summit.org/resources/videos/good -god-allow-hell/.

15. Tony Evans, *Oneness Embraced: Reconciliation, the Kingdom, and How We Are Stronger Together* (Chicago: Moody, 2011), 251.

Chapter 9

1. Larry Norman, vocalist, "I Wish We'd All Been Ready," by Larry Norman, track 9 on *Upon This Rock*, Capitol Records, 1969.

2. Jim Reeves, "This World Is Not My Home," on *We Thank Thee*, RCA Records, 1962.

3. "This World Has Nothing for Me," Reddit, 2016, www.reddit.com/r/SuicideWatch /comments/40rg1k/this_world_has_nothing_for_me.

4. Desperation Band, "Rescue," by Jared Anderson, track 15 on *Light Up the World*, Integrity Music, 2009.

5. Caedmon's Call, "This World," by Aaron Tate, track 2 on *My Calm, Your Storm*, 1994.

6. Michael Allen Williams, *Rethinking "Gnosticism": An Argument for Dismantling a Dubious Category* (Princeton, NJ: Princeton University Press, 1996), 52; Rodney Stark, *Cities of God: The Real Story of How Christianity Became an Urban Movement and Conquered Rome* (New York: HarperOne, 2007), 146–48.

7. Irenaeus, *Against Heresies*, 1.30.9, quoted in Williams, *Rethinking "Gnosticism,"* 121.

8. Jonathan Hill, *The History of Christian Thought: The Fascinating Story of the Great Christian Thinkers and How They Helped Shape the World as We Know It Today* (Downers Grove, IL: IVP Academic, 2003), 27.

9. Justo L. Gonzalez, *From the Beginnings to the Council of Chalcedon*, rev. ed., A History of Christian Thought, vol. 1 (Nashville: Abingdon, 1987), 151–56. The Apostles' Creed reads as follows: "I believe in God the Father Almighty, maker of heaven and earth: and in Jesus Christ his only Son our Lord, who was conceived by the Holy Ghost, born of the Virgin Mary, suffered under Pontius Pilate, was crucified, dead, and buried: he descended into hell; the third day he rose again from the dead; he ascended into heaven, and sitteth on the right hand of God the Father Almighty; from thence he shall come to judge the quick and the dead. I believe in the Holy Ghost, the holy catholic church, the communion of saints, the forgiveness of sins, the resurrection of the body, and the life everlasting. Amen."

10. Christian thinker Francis Schaeffer (1912–84) made this point in his many books, especially *How Should We Then Live? The Rise and Decline of Western Thought and Culture* (1976; repr., Wheaton, IL: Crossway Books, 2005).

11. Jacques Berlinerblau, *How to Be Secular: A Call to Arms for Religious Freedom* (New York: Houghton Mifflin Harcourt, 2012), 180.

12. Lord Melbourne, quoted in Kevin White, "Bridging the Divide: A Brief History of Sacred versus Secular," Business as Mission, April 29, 2015, http://businessasmission.com/bridging-the-divide.

13. "Share the Big Story," InterVarsity Evangelism, accessed August 28, 2019, http://evangelism.intervarsity.org/resource/share-big-story.

14. Glenn Sunshine, "Krishna Mohan Bannerjee (1813–1885)," BreakPoint, March 25, 2013, www.breakpoint.org/2013/03/krishna-mohan-bannerjee-1813-1885.

15. Henry Wadsworth Longfellow, "Flower-de-Luce (Collection)/Christmas Bells," Wikisource, accessed September 16, 2019, https://en.wikisource.org/wiki/Flower-de-Luce_(Collection)/Christmas_Bells.

16. Charles C. Calhoun, *Longfellow: A Rediscovered Life* (Boston: Beacon, 2004), 215–16.

17. Abraham Lincoln, "Annual Message to Congress: Concluding Remarks" (speech, Washington, DC, December 1, 1862), www.abrahamlincolnonline.org/lincoln/speeches/congress.htm.

18. Longfellow, "Flower-de-Luce (Collection)/Christmas Bells."

19. Richard John Neuhaus, "Telling the World Its Own Story," Catholic Education Resource Center, July 2001, www.catholiceducation.org/en/religion-and-philosophy/apologetics/telling-the-world-its-own-story.html.

20. Longfellow, "Flower-de-Luce (Collection)/Christmas Bells."

Chapter 10

1. George Herbert, "The Flower," in *George Herbert: The Complete Poetry*, ed. John Drury and Victoria Moul (London: Penguin Books, 2015), 158.

2. Kara Powell and Brad M. Griffin, "I Doubt It: Making Space for Hard Questions," Fuller Youth Institute, March 10, 2014, https://fulleryouthinstitute.org/articles/i-doubt-it.

3. "God Is So Good," Hymnary.com, public domain, accessed September 16, 2019, https://hymnary.org/hymn/LUYH2013/777.

4. R. J. Rummel, *Death by Government* (New Brunswick, NJ: Transaction, 1994).

5. Nelson Mandela, "Speech by President Nelson Mandela at the Launch of the Nelson Mandela Children's Fund" (speech, Pretoria, South Africa, May 8, 1995), http://db.nelsonmandela.org/speeches/pub_view.asp?pg=item&itemid =nmS250&txtstr=mahla.

6. In his interview with graduate student Nick Trakakis, William Rowe not only revealed why he believes the problem of evil disproves God's existence but also explained how he went from being a fundamentalist Christian enrolled in Bible college to being an atheist. William Rowe, interview by Nick Trakakis, *Philosophy Now*, August/September 2004, https://philosophynow.org/issues /47/William_Rowe.

7. Stephen Mitchell, trans., *Bhagavad Gita: A New Translation* (New York: Three Rivers, 2000), 47. Krishna's statement represents the general tenor of Hindu writing on evil and suffering, though Hinduism is a very diverse religion and not all Hindus hold this view of suffering. Hinduism is actually a religious culture that, according to Taylor University professor emeritus of philosophy and religion Winfried Corduan, "has moved back and forth through various phases of monotheism, henotheism, polytheism and animism, with each stage retaining at least a vestigial presence in the ensuing one. There is no set of core beliefs that remains constant throughout. The name itself, actually a label devised by Westerners, simply means 'the religion of India.'" *Neighboring Faiths: A Christian Introduction to World Religions*, 2nd ed. (Downers Grove, IL: IVP Academic, 2012), 267. See also R. C. Zaehner, *Hinduism* (Oxford: Oxford University Press, 1966).

8. Walpola Sri Rahula, "The First Sermon of the Buddha," *Tricycle*, accessed August 29, 2019, https://tricycle.org/magazine/the-first-sermon-of-the -buddha.

9. For a helpful explication of this doctrine amid challenges of open theism, see William Lane Craig's very readable book *What Does God Know? Reconciling Divine Foreknowledge and Human Freedom* (Norcross, GA: RZIM, 2002).

10. Thanks to R. Scott Smith for articulating this point: *In Search of Moral Knowledge: Overcoming the Fact-Value Dichotomy* (Downers Grove, IL: InterVarsity, 2014). See also Udo Middelmann, *The Innocence of God* (Downers Grove, IL: Biblica Books, 2007), 134.

11. Michael Bauman, "Augustine and Pelagius" (lecture, Student Conference, Summit Ministries, Manitou Springs, CO, June 13, 2019).

12. William Lane Craig, *Divine Foreknowledge and Human Freedom: The Coherence of Theism: Omniscience* (Leiden, Netherlands: E. J. Brill, 1991), 238–46, 268–72. Craig argued for a position called Molinism," which was first articulated by a Jesuit priest named Luis de Molina (1535–1600). Molina proposed a middle-knowledge view of God that avoided the idea that God directly causes every action in the universe (divine determinism) and also its opposite extreme, open theism, that while God is knowledgeable enough to make very accurate guesses about what will and won't happen in the future, he does not know it with certainty.

13. Norman L. Geisler, *If God, Why Evil? A New Way to Think about the Question* (Bloomington, MN: Bethany, 2011), 19. Augustine discussed the problem of evil at length in *Confessions*, book 7, which is available free online at www.ccel.org/a/augustine/confessions/confessions.html.

14. Geisler, *If God, Why Evil?*, 30–31.

15. I'm afraid this is an embarrassingly simplistic summary of philosopher Alvin Plantinga's defense of free will. Plantinga was not trying to definitively *state the reason* God allows evil. To do that, he would have to know the mind of God. Rather, he was offering an explanation for why it might be so. To those who say, "There is no explanation," Plantinga was replying, "Here is a possible one." Even if his explanation is faulty, it nonetheless demonstrates that the argument "There is *no* explanation" is invalid. See Alvin C. Plantinga, *God, Freedom, and Evil* (Grand Rapids, MI: Eerdmans, 1977), 30.

16. This summary necessarily leaves out many nuances of the argument for free will. Readers wishing to study the argument in more detail are especially directed to, in addition to the other resources from this chapter, Plantinga's *God, Freedom, and Evil.*

17. Randy Alcorn, *If God Is Good: Faith in the Midst of Suffering and Evil* (Colorado Springs: Multnomah, 2009), 449.

18. Larry Crabb, *Shattered Dreams: God's Unexpected Path to Joy* (Colorado Springs: WaterBrook, 2001), 1.

ABOUT SUMMIT MINISTRIES

Summit Ministries exists to see generations of Christians mobilized to transform a broken world. We do this by training rising generations to understand how to navigate culture through truth and relationship. Through two-week conferences for students, Christian school and homeschool Bible curriculum, fall semester programs, and thousands of resources online and in print, we help the next generation see how the Bible is more than a historical book. Summit helps students see that Christianity provides a full picture to understand reality. It's not just a personal conviction, but a worldview. At Summit, we equip Christians who seek to pass the baton of faithfulness to the next generation.

Find out more about how you can engage at summit.org.

WORLDVIEW CONFERENCES

Summit Student Conferences take place each summer for two weeks. These conferences challenge students, ages 16-25, to think deeper about their personal faith and convictions. Students learn and engage with today's top worldview thinkers and apologists as they dive into the topics of life, identity, leadership, and many more relevant issues.

After attending Summit's worldview conference your students will be able to meaningfully influence culture by:

- Understanding the Bible and applying it personally and in their vocations
- Refuting false worldviews
- Promoting the value of life
- Embracing a biblical view of family and sexuality
- Respecting America's heritage
- Championing economic freedom

Explore upcoming locations and dates at summit.org/students.

Want to dig deeper?

Find additional content for each chapter in *Unquestioned Answers*, including videos and additional study questions by visiting:

www.unquestionedanswers.com

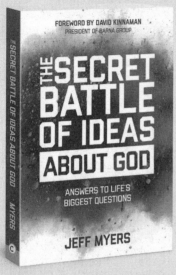